MODEL REALISTIC FREIGHT CAR LOADS

Keith M. Kohlmann

About the author: Keith Kohlmann has written more than 100 articles on prototype and model railroading subjects for *Model Railroader, Railroad Model Craftsman,* and other hobby and historical society publications. He is an active N scale modeler with a specific interest in mid-20th century railroads and the industrial heritage of the upper Midwest. He is an avid researcher of railroad and industrial subjects and a popular presenter at civic and railroad historical societies and prototype modeling conferences. He enjoys many facets of the hobby, especially building historic rolling stock, structures, and modules for outdoor photography and display.

Keith worked as a section foreman in the engineering department of the Chicago & North Western before completing a master's degree in industrial and technical education from the University of Wisconsin-Stout. He has been teaching industrial arts and writing for 30 years.

Acknowledgements: This book was only made possible with the help of all the photographers, researchers, authors, and organizers who contribute to the prototype modeling community. I would like to thank the many people who assisted by providing photographs and information including: Bob Baker, Bob Bender, Jeff Eggert, Tom Farrell, Bob Gallegos, Cody Grivno, Doug Harding, Damon Hassell, Lloyd Keyser, Vince Kotnik, John Luckfield, Greg Mross, Dave Nelson, Mary Kay Mandli Nelson, Jim Podlich, Ron Poniatowski, Clark Probst, Bill Schaumburg, Keith Schmidt, Dave Sima, Jeff Wilson, and all the photographers whose work resides in the David P. Morgan Library at Kalmbach Media.

On the cover: An overhead crane loads several Minneapolis-Moline Jet Star 3 tractors aboard Great Northern flatcars at the M-M factory in Minneapolis in the early 1960s. *Great Northern*

Back cover: Models of an N scale gondola with coiled wire load and a flatcar carrying street sweepers are being switched. *Keith Kohlmann* A small vertical stationary boiler is blocked and secured to a Central of Georgia flatcar in the early 1960s.
J. David Ingles

Kalmbach Media
21027 Crossroads Circle
Waukesha, Wisconsin 53186
www.KalmbachHobbyStore.com

Published in 2022
26 25 24 23 22 1 2 3 4 5

Manufactured in China

ISBN: 978-1-62700-884-6
EISBN: 978-1-62700-885-3

Editor: Jeff Wilson
Book Design: Lisa Bergman

Library of Congress Control Number: 2021948320

Contents

Several Elin 250-ton transformers have been transferred from a ship to heavy-duty depressed center flatcars at the Port of Milwaukee on April 16, 2005. The transformers were imported from Europe as part of a large wind-energy installation in Iowa. *Keith Kohlmann*

CHAPTER ONE

Steel, metal products, and scrap

Steel products come in many shapes and forms; this TTJX bulkhead flat has been converted to carry coiled wire. Angled bunks with wooden contact surfaces support the coils, which have strapping and wire ties. Polyester strapping is threaded through the coils and secured by the ratchets on the side sills. The TTX Co. operates a wide variety of flatcars to carry many types of loads. *Cody Grivno*

Steel and other metal products are among the major commodities shipped by rail as open-top loads. These include ingots, sheet steel, coiled steel, beams, rods, wire, and other forms, **1**. Steel fabricating companies use this material to produce vehicles, boilers, fencing, roofing, siding, bridges, auto parts, machinery, appliances, pipes, consumer products, and much more.

St. Louis Southwestern bulkhead flat car 875776 passes through Butler Yard outside Milwaukee, Wis., on Aug. 30, 2003. It carries steel plate resting on 4x4 wood stringers. Heavy steel banding secured to the stake pockets and across the top of the load is pulled tight by threaded steel rods. *Vince Kotnik*

Baltimore & Ohio gondola 356524 has been modified to carry wide steel plates as seen at Toledo, Ohio in October 1990. This load appears to be around 5" thick and is far too wide to carry flat on a car. The supports were made from I-beams that are designed to support plates of two different widths.
Keith Kohlmann collection

A bulkhead flat car is loaded with bundled aluminum rods at Galesburg, Ill., in June 2011. The deck has raised bunks and chains to tie down the load. Polyester banding and wooden separators run throughout the load. An identical formation rests on the opposite end of the car. *Dave Nelson*

These loads originate at steel mills and ports (for imported steel) located throughout the country. Specialized mini-mills serve specific local markets. Steel leaves the mills in many forms: plate, bars, rebar, beams, rails, pipe, wire, angles, channels, columns, tees, and zees. The most common form is sheet steel, and it is shipped in coils. All of these products must be shipped safely and all require different securement techniques due to the differences in length, weight, and volume of the items. American Association of Railroads (AAR) rules provide instructions for loading all common types of steel products.

Types of steel loads

Steel plate is large sheet material ¼" or thicker that can't be coiled. It is shipped flat and secured with heavy steel banding placed over the top of the load and looped through the stake pockets. Sheets are stacked and bundled together with banding. The individual bundles are then banded to each other, **2**. Wood 2x4s separate the bundles for ease of handling. Steel plate can be flat, perforated, or diamond pattern. Steel plate wider than a flatcar deck is shipped diagonally in gondolas equipped with racks, **3**. Steel plate can be up to 6" thick.

Loads of steel rods and bars are also common. Rods, **4**, have a round cross section and bars have a square or rectangular cross section, **5**. They are shipped in banded bundles. Wooden separators are placed beneath the load and between the layers of bundles. Wooden separators are also placed along the sides of gondolas to prevent surface damage to the bundles. Bundles of rebar (short for "reinforcing bar") are shipped in gondolas or on specialized Trailer-Train flat cars equipped with vertical steel "fingers" that separate and support the bundles.

5

Wooden 4x5 boards separate the layers of steel bundles in this gondola load. Wood is also placed against the sides of the car and on the floor to protect the load from shifting and vibration. The floors in some gondolas are covered in dirt, scrap metal, broken wood, and trash. This is at Galesburg, Ill., in 2011.
Dave Nelson

6

A Railgon gondola is spotted under a Mi-Jack Travelift 500-B rubber-tired gantry crane at a team track in Mitchell Yard at Milwaukee in 2005. The crane is used to transfer bundled steel from gondolas to flatbed trucks for local distribution.
Keith Kohlmann

Rebar can be a natural steel color or covered in corrosion-resistant paint. All of these components are loaded and unloaded by cranes, **6**.

Steel beams have cross sections resembling the letters I, H, Z, L, or T. The shapes are cut to various lengths, which determine the length of the flat car or mill gondola they are shipped in. A load might contain more than one variety, and different lengths, depending on what a customer ordered from the mill, **7**. They are secured with bands (often bundled), with wood between the components to keep them from getting dented or dinged.

Railroad rails today are produced in standard 78-foot lengths, and they typically are carried on long flatcars outfitted with bulkheads and steel side stakes, **8**. Prior to the 1970s, rail was typically delivered in 39-foot lengths, allowing sections to be loaded in 40-foot general-service gondolas. Welded ("ribbon") rail is shipped in ¼-mile-long sections on specialized ribbon-rail cars and trains.

Bridge (plate) girders are fabricated from plate steel and angle stock, either riveted or welded together, **9**. A factory that makes girders is a great choice for a trackside industry that uses open loads. Inbound loads of sheet steel and beams are unloaded and stacked under an electric overhead traveling crane, and outbound finished girders are

7

This TTX bulkhead flat carries a load of nested H-beams. Each layer is secured with heavy steel strapping and separated by wooden blocks. Stub stakes support the sides of the load. Note that some of the bands have snapped, and the load has shifted while in transit on the Union Pacific in Nebraska in 2006. *Jeff Wilson*

8

New rail today is typically delivered in 78-foot lengths. This Colorado & Wyoming car is typical of flats in rail service. It's an 89-foot former piggyback car that's had short bulkheads and side stakes added, allowing the rail load to ride without additional restraints. It's on the BNSF in August 2016. *Jeff Wilson*

9

Five flat cars are required to move two steel girders that are each nearly 100 feet long. Threaded steel rods secure this girder to QTTX flat no. 132045. Anchors have been welded to the flat car's steel deck to secure the rods. The girder rests on thick hardwood beams that raise the girder above the decks of the adjacent idler flat cars. They're at Franklin Park, Ill., in 2009. *Dave Sima*

This pair of trusses dwarfs the 65-foot mill gondola in which they're loaded, with idler cars at each end, in this 1964 scene. Steel angles secure the trusses at three points on the car, with additional steel cables at each end; the girders rest on heavy wood blocks. *John Ingles; J. David Ingles collection*

Three large steel coils are a full load for this Elgin, Joliet & Eastern gondola at Galesburg, Ill., in 2003. The specially marked white end of the car is stenciled "COIL LOADING ONLY." These cars are modified with V-shaped troughs running the length of the car floors. A coil steel car with covers is at left. *Dave Nelson*

placed on flat cars or in drop-end mill gondolas. Girders are shipped upright, with blocking under each end and steel rods running from the side pockets to the top of the girder to secure it. Long girders often require idler flat cars on both ends of the load (the load does not contact the idler cars).

Trusses are structural assemblies made with steel beams, **10**, most often used as structural roof supports. They are loaded in mill gondolas in the same manner as plate girders, with idler flats on either end of extra-long loads.

Coiled steel is thin sheet steel used in auto-parts stamping plants, appliance factories, pipe mills, and many other industries. It is produced in a strip mill. Thin, continuous sheets of steel (and other metals) are rolled into tight coils held together by steel banding, **11**. In the 1950s a usual shipment was four coils strapped into a gondola modified for coil service with wooden cradles built into the floor, **12**. The coils were placed in the cradle, resting against the ends of the car. By the early 1960s covers were placed over some gondolas to protect the coils from the elements. Gondolas are still often used for coils, but various designs of specialized covered coil cars began appearing in the mid-1960s. These are most often operated with covers, but sometimes run open, **13**.

This overhead view of an EJ&E coil gondola at Grand Avenue in Milwaukee in 1988 shows the longitudinal wooden trough built inside the car. Gravity holds the coils in place—other than the trough, there is no blocking securing the coils. The car is littered with steel banding from previous loads. The coils are identified with stenciled codes and paint markers. *Vince Kotnik*

Pennsylvania no. 387177 is a G41A coil car, an early (1960s) design. The covers have been removed for this shipment of seven steel coils. Adjustable braces wedge the coil into the floor and walls of the car to keep the coil from moving. The car was outside a steel mill in Cleveland on April 23, 1990. *John C. Benson*

14

This Canadian National bulkhead flat car pauses with a load of aluminum ingots fresh out of the Alcan smelter outside the port facilities at La Baie, Quebec, on June 26, 1993. Adjustable clamps on the deck of the car brace the banded ingots. *Keith Kohlmann collection*

15

A crew of oilfield workers unloads 10" re-lay oil pipe from a Nickel Plate Road mill gondola on a siding near Kilgore, Tex., in 1950. Side stakes that support the load were made from sapling trees. *Keith Kohlmann collection*

16

This mill gondola is loaded with 40-foot pipe at Dunvegan Yard in Edmonton, Alberta, in 1972. The load, which has shifted a bit from slack action, is supported by wooden 4x4 side stakes wired together over the top of the load. The pipes are banded together and separated by 2x4 spacers. *Keith Kohlmann collection*

Ingots are bars or blocks of relatively pure metal intended for further processing. They can be shipped in open cars to manufacturing plants for shaping, rolling, cutting, or milling to produce a variety of final products. Ingots are placed loosely on wooden spacers inside gondolas or strapped to bulkhead flat cars, **14**. Loads of light-density metal, such as aluminum, can be relatively large; denser metal, such as steel, will reach a car's weight limit with what looks like a small load.

Steel pipe is used by the utility, construction, and oil and gas industries, **15**. Pipes are made in various diameters and lengths from steel, cast iron, clay, plastic, fiberglass, and wood. Each type is loaded a bit differently as an open load on a flat car or gondola, **16**. Steel pipes are painted black or will be a raw steel color with slight rusting. Coated pipes can be red, blue, green, or yellow with the uncoated ends a rust color. The AAR rules for loading show steel pipes braced with wooden side stakes supported by layers of banding running through the stacked or nested pipes, **17**.

Cast iron and clay pipes are fragile. Their flared ends alternate in the stack, and wooden separators help stabilize the load and protect the pipes, **18**, so the pipes don't rest directly upon each other. Layers of banding keep the load together.

Long-distance pipelines are constructed from 80-foot lengths of pipe, **19**. These are shipped on 89-foot

17 **The end detail of the steel pipe load at left includes black polyester straps surrounding the entire load, with 1x4 wooden separator boards with triangle-shaped 4x4 blocks to cradle the load and hold the pipes in alignment. Each pipe has a paper identification tag clipped to the end. The gondola load of pipes at right, at Techny, Ill., in 2012, is supported by 10 2x4 upright stakes. The gondola sides keep the stakes in position, and they're supported horizontally by steel straps running across the top of the load and through the layers of pipes. Steel wire binds each layer of pipes to the one above it.** *Left: Keith Kohlmann; right: Dave Nelson*

18 **This PTTX flat car is set up to carry cast iron pipe at Galesburg, Ill., in 2013. Steel channels are welded across the deck of the car which hold 6x6 timbers. Cast iron is easily damaged in transit, so the layers are separated by wooden blocking. Polyester straps keep the stacked pipes together and secure them to the deck.** *Dave Nelson*

flat cars (converted piggyback cars) and secured with polyester straps tightened by the ratchets mounted on the side sills of the cars, **20**.

Flexible plastic pipe is generally wound on large spools for shipping. Since it is relatively lightweight, several spools are generally loaded aboard a long flatcar for shipping, **21**.

Coiled wire is produced by wire mills from heated steel billets that are drawn through successively smaller dies. The wire is wound into rolls, banded, and loaded into gondolas, **22**, **1**, or wound on spools and loaded on bulkhead flat cars equipped with bunks and ratchet tie-down equipment. Coiled wire is shipped to all kinds of metalworking industries for further processing into finished products—everything from paper clips to car parts. High-value wire (such as copper) is generally shipped as a covered load.

Scrap metal

Scrap steel is a basic raw material of iron and steel production. It can be

The nine plastic coated pipes on PTTX 136501 are held together at multiple levels with polyester strapping. Wood separators support the lower layers, while the upper layers are nested together. It's at Dayton's Bluff at St. Paul, Minn., in 2019. *Bob Bender*

Wooden separators are contoured to support this load just out of the pipe mill at Camrose, Alberta, in 2019. Tightened ratchet winches on the side sills secure the load with polyester straps. The pipes are coated with corrosion-resistant material, but the ends of the pipe are uncoated where they will be welded together. Identification information is stenciled inside the pipes. *Keith Kohlmann*

Seven reels of flexible plastic pipe are secured to an ITTX flatcar rolling through Granite City, Ill., in 2015. Chains with tensioners lock the reels to the channels in the deck of the car. *Bob Gallegos*

AAR loading diagrams

The American Association of Railroads (AAR) has published a wide variety of diagrams and instructions on loading and securing steel components and various other materials in open-top cars. The following chapters include a few samples. Specific guidelines and requirements have changed from the steam era through today as loads have changed (and gotten bigger), freight cars have become more specialized, and securing and banding materials have evolved and improved. Twisted wire has largely given way to steel cables (and built-in cables/ratchets), semi-permanent chains with tie-down hooks, and steel banding.

The tremendous variety of loads and AAR diagrams makes it impossible to cover them in detail here (the section on military loads alone is more than 100 pages long), but fortunately for modelers and railfans the AAR publishes these guides online. You can see them at my.aar.org/OTLR; many include detailed diagrams that show blocking and strapping requirements. These are an excellent resource for modeling.

The Southern gondola (above) is loaded with coiled wire. Individual coils are banded, but they are stacked loosely in the car. Woven wire rope can also be shipped on large spools as on the Great Northern cars at right. The spools are blocked with wood beams and tied down at the centers to the side pockets. Wood strips surround each spool, banded in place. *Above: Vince Kotnik; right: N.F. Priebe*

23

Some scrap yards are vast outdoor materials processing facilities with extensive trackage to various balers, docks, piles, and loading areas for each type of scrap. Here Miller Compressing in Milwaukee is operating extended-cab locomotive cranes to move and load gondolas at the South Water Street Yard in June 2005. Cuts of cars are delivered and picked up by the local railroad on an interchange track at the entrance to the yard, but the railroad crew does not switch cars in the biggest yards. The locomotive cranes do all the switching inside the plant, then they spot the cars back out on the interchange track for pickup. During an operating session, one operator could be assigned to run the self-propelled scrapyard crane, keeping the local switch crews busy spotting the interchange. *Keith Kohlmann*

the byproduct of manufacturing or anything that has become obsolete, discarded, or recycled. Scrap metal of many types (steel, iron, copper, brass, aluminum, etc.) comes from factories, households, railroads, utilities, shipyards, demolition sites, and salvage yards—anywhere metal products are made or used. This material is remelted and recycled.

Railroads transport scrap metal to mills and docks in open gondolas. However, scrap cannot be immediately used in its original form. It must be sorted using chemical analysis (there are many variations of each type of metal, based on the percentage of various alloys). The scrap is then sorted and processed before it can be remelted. Scrap metal can be seen traveling by rail in open loads between scrapyards, factories, and mills. Scrap is also often transloaded into barges at riverfront docks and onto ocean-going vessels at ports along the coasts and on the Great Lakes, **23**.

There are dozens of types of scrap metal and scrap metal loads, but for the sake of simplicity, I've reduced these classifications to the following, based on the outward appearance of an open load, **24**.

Heavy remelt steel is the most common type of scrap, and is defined as industrial or commercial scrap steel thicker than ⅛", such as plates, beams, and channels. It may include scrap machinery such as railroad, farm, and construction equipment, steel castings, and certain types of stampings. Processed material must be no longer than 5 feet and no wider than 18". Large pieces and assemblies are reduced in size with hydraulic shears or cutting torches. Depending on the steel mill, this scrap may eventually need to be cut to a smaller maximum dimension of 1 foot. It is loaded loosely into gondolas for shipping, **25**.

24

No two open carloads of mixed scrap look alike. Engine blocks, demolition debris, broken machines, structural shapes, sheet metal, and cast iron were separated into each of these gondolas seen at Milwaukee in 1994. *Dave Nelson*

This is a Thrall rotary dump coal gondola that has been repurposed to haul scrap for J.M. Bastille Acier Inc., based in Rivière-du-Loup, Quebec. Surplus coal gondolas can be found hauling scrap metal, used ties, and debris. *Bob Bender*

Not all scrap metal is rust-colored. This loaded gondola has white, green, red, and yellow-painted metal visible among rusty parts that range in color from dark brown to light orange. *Dave Nelson*

Scrap turnings and borings have been loaded into this Chicago & North Western gondola. The crane operator left impressions of the electromagnet where it was used to pack the gondola more tightly. The car is being switched at Milwaukee in 1994. *Dave Nelson*

Pressing steel is mixed household scrap up to ¼" thick, sometimes called "white goods," **26**. This includes stoves, refrigerators, washing machines, bicycles, water tanks, furnaces, metal furniture, sheet-metal roofing, and sheet-metal cut-offs. This post-consumer material is frequently brought to local scrapyards where it is sorted and compressed into 20" cubes.

Cast iron includes machinery, engine blocks, pipe, and bathtubs. This material must be broken into chunks not larger than 24 x 30 inches, with no pieces weighing more than 150 pounds. Scrap processors break up heavy cast iron by dropping a heavy wrecking ball on the item.

Turnings and borings are fine metal chips cast off during machining.

28

This N scale car carries crushed automobiles from a small local scrap yard in an early 1950s scene. The salvage yard didn't have a baling machine, so the autos were flattened, then secured with wire and scrap wood for shipping to a larger dealer for processing. This once-common loading technique is no longer allowed under AAR rules. The gondola is a modified Intermountain kit; the resin crushed auto load is from Fine N Scale. *Keith Kohlmann*

Scrapyards collect chips from multiple sources to get a full carload. Certain piles within a scrapyard might be dedicated to a particular alloy from a local manufacturer. Before cuttings can be shipped to a steel mill, the cutting oil on this material must be drained and collected, otherwise the oil may heat and combust—this can cause a gondola filled with borings to smolder and reach temperatures near the melting point. Gondolas are often seen with the paint burned off the sides where the heat in a load of borings became too intense. Turnings are loaded level with the top of the gondola and may appear to have a blue, silver, or rust color. They are packed into gondolas with electromagnets. **27**.

29

Baled stainless steel scrap metal rides in this gondola at Galesburg, Ill., in 2014. The bales are marked with orange spray paint. Scrap yards separate and process different types of scrap for remelting. *Dave Nelson*

Automobile bodies are another common type of scrap. Vehicles of all kinds are made of sheet metal, including automobiles, buses, trucks, and trolley cars, and they must be processed (with parts sorted) before they can be crushed or shredded. Gasoline, oil, batteries, mercury switches, and valuable and toxic metals must be removed before the vehicles can be crushed. Larger vehicles are cut into pieces with a torch or shears. Some are ripped apart by hydraulic materials handlers. Smaller yards that did not have compressing equipment used crane magnets to smash auto bodies as flat as they could get them. Then the autos were stacked well above the sides of a gondola fitted with temporary wooden side extensions, **28**. The crushed autos could also be loaded standing up in bulkhead gondolas leaning against the ends. The loads were shipped to a larger yard where the cars could be compressed into bales. Most large salvage yards now shred automobiles into uniform-sized metal chips. This facilitates the separation of different metals and plastic waste.

Baled steel is created when scrap is sorted, compressed, and baled. The

This Chicago & North Western burro crane loads scrap rail with a magnet into a gondola at Carrollville, Wis., in July 1990. Scrap rail has marks where the tie plates were in contact with the base of the rail. It is often torch-cut to random lengths and not stacked carefully inside the gondola the way re-lay rail (rail intended for re-use) is loaded. *Keith Kohlmann*

A switchman rides a gondola through the interchange at Ackerville, Wis., in March 2016. The gondola is loaded with scrap freight car wheels heading to a Chicago-area steel mill. Scrap wheels are removed from the axles before they are sent to the mill. *Dave Nelson*

The sad remains of Milwaukee Road no. 251, a Class S-1 4-8-4 Northern, are switched at Chicago in 1955. The running gear was removed at the railroad shops. The boiler and cab are supported on the deck of the flat car by heavy timbers and steel banding. *Keith Kohlmann collection*

resulting cubes (called "one-and-a-half bundles") are loaded into gondolas, **29**. The cubes should not be loaded higher than the sides of the car. The load then heads to a steel mill for remelting. Some crane operators take the time to carefully arrange the cubes in the gondola. Others drop the cubes into the car at random. Baled scrap operations are being replaced by shredding at the largest scrap processors.

Railroad scrap comprises several materials. Worn-out rails are removed by maintenance-of-way crews, **30**. This valuable scrap is sent to contractors or scrapyards that cut the rail into 36" sections with hydraulic shears before selling it to a steel mill. Old spikes, tie plates, joint bars, and track appliances are sent directly to a steel mill. Railroad steel is kept separate from other scrap steel because railroad steel has a greater purity. It has less copper contamination and is in high demand. Worn-out wheels are removed from their axles and loaded into a gondola for scrapping, **31**.

Retired steam locomotive boilers were secured on flatcars for shipment to scrapyards, **32**. Each railroad had a method for disposing of steam locomotives. Many were sold to scrap dealers that cut them up off railroad property. After shop forces salvaged appliances and the parts that could be rebuilt or re-used, the Milwaukee Road shops cut scrap locomotives and shipped them in gondolas to scrap yards for further processing, **33**. Old wood-body and composite passenger and freight cars were burned to free metal parts from wood, and the metal parts then cut up and loaded as scrap. Steel cars were cut into large sections which were sent to scrap yards for further processing. Higher value scrap, such as copper wire, brass bearings, manganese alloy points, frogs, and track diamonds were cut into smaller pieces and shipped in enclosed boxcars.

Mixed scrap is a random load of assorted iron and steel items, often collected by a small scrapyard, heading to a larger scrapyard for sorting and processing. These gondolas could be loaded by hand or with a small crane.

33

This mill gondola holds the left side of the carbody of Milwaukee Road FP7 98C at Davies Yard in Milwaukee in June 1976. It, and the remains of a Fairbanks-Morse H16-44 switcher in the trailing car (top photo), are on their way to a scrap yard. The photo above shows how the locomotive was cut in half to allow it to fit inside the gondola. Retired locomotives and freight cars sometimes traveled to scrapyards on their own wheels; other times, like this, they are cut apart and loaded aboard gondolas. *Two photos: Rod Robinson; Keith Kohlmann collection*

34

This Chicago & North Western general-service gon arrived with a rather haphazard load of mixed scrap metal for processing at Consumer's Steel and Supply Co. at Racine Junction, Wis., in September 1977. This load violates AAR rules because several large pieces are stacked above the top of the car, and they are not secured with wire or braced with side stakes. *Keith Kohlmann*

If the load was not very dense, wooden side extensions could be added so more items could be loaded into the car. These are interesting (and sometimes frightening-looking) open loads because of their haphazard appearance. Carelessly loaded cars were dangerous to crews because scrap metal hanging over the side of the car could strike a worker on the ground or someone riding on an adjacent car, locomotive, or caboose, **34**.

A scrap processing yard will receive a wide variety of materials, including auto bodies, machinery, appliances, turnings, tin cans, and demolition

35

This N scale Micro-Trains mill gondola carries a Micro-Engineering bridge girder loaded according to AAR rules Basswood blocks are placed under the girder to raise it above the idler flatcar decks at each end. Piano-wire supports are secured between the blocks above, below, and on the ends of the girders. All bracing was glued to the girder to make it a single removable assembly. *Keith Kohlmann*

36

This HO scale pipe load rides in a Proto 2000 mill gondola. Jeff Wilson made it from soda straws glued together and spray-painted brown. The banding is E-Z Line; stripwood represents the vertical stakes and cross pieces. The stakes are glued to the load instead of the car, making it removable. *Jeff Wilson*

scrap. These materials are all processed and will leave for the steel mill in gondolas as smaller pieces of metal (shred) or as compressed cubes (one-and-a-half bundles). Some scrapyards will salvage pipe, beams, and bar stock for re-use.

Scrapyards are part of the materials processing industry, and they are also commodities brokers, managing their inventories for maximum profit. During periods where prices are low, a scrapyard may stockpile inventory temporarily waiting for prices to go up or stockpile scrap as a service to their customers. Mountains of various grades of processed scrap metal represent valuable inventory in a scrapyard.

Most scrapyards also collect and process non-ferrous metals such as aluminum, brass, copper, and lead. These higher-value metals are shipped in trailers or boxcars. If there is a strong supply in the area, a scrap dealer might also collect paper, cardboard, and rags in nearby buildings.

Modeling steel loads

Steel products can be modeled using brass or styrene strips, shapes, tubes, and sheets that are cut to size, bundled, and painted to resemble steel. Gunmetal, dark gray, black, and rust colors can be blended to achieve a realistic load. Rust-colored chalk can be dusted over the edges of the load.

Build each load by gluing the painted and bundled shapes together in the same way the prototype would build the load. To be realistic, it's important to follow prototype practice. There's no way to provide guidelines for all situations, as every load tends to vary a bit, and even identical loads may be handled in different fashion by multiple railroads or shippers. Your best bet is to follow photographs and the AAR diagrams available on-line (see "AAR Loading Diagrams" on page 13). Prototype photos are often the best guide, as you can copy what you see, and many photos are available online and in books. Photos also show how railroads have changed their methods of securing various types of loads over the years.

Add wooden separators between layers. Stripwood is available in a wide range of sizes; again, follow AAR guides for sizes, or estimate the sizes based on photographs. Glue on strapping or banding, which can be made from heavy E-Z Line (a flexible thread made by Berkshire Junction), thread, or chart tape. Scale chain is made by A-Line, Campbell, ModelTech Studios, and others. Brass wire from Detail Associates can simulate steel rods and wire tie-downs.

For added flexibility, design the load to be a single assembly that is removable. Scenic Accents glue will keep loads in place on freight cars, and it allows for easy removal and repositioning of items.

Fabricated bridge girders can be

This N scale scene shows an open load of coiled wire and a load of Elgin "Street King" sweepers in a late-1950s scene. The sweepers are kits from Brian Feddorf with custom decals made on a laser printer. The loads were secured with basswood blocking and E-Z Line following AAR loading rules. The wire is modeled with curly gray doll hair glued to a styrene false floor in rows with matte medium. *Keith Kohlmann*

modeled in all scales using parts from Atlas, Central Valley, Micro-Engineering, or Walthers bridge kits, **35**. Paint the girder orange, black, green, gray, or oxide red. Some girders have the name of the manufacturer, either on a paper sign or stenciled on the girder. Center the girder in the car, resting on a thick hardwood beam placed over each bolster. Drill holes for the wire rods that will support the load. The angled wooden or steel rod supports are glued to styrene straps that wrap over the top of the girder. Make sure the load doesn't touch the decks of the idler cars on either end.

This N scale gondola is loaded with heavy-remelt scrap steel. A Micro-Trains composite gondola was enhanced by gluing separate bits of painted scrap over the Micro-Trains resin scrap load insert. *Keith Kohlmann*

Inexpensive model pipe loads can be constructed by gluing together layers of drinking straws (or brass or plastic tubing), painting it an appropriate color, then securing it to the car with and stripwood, **36**, and finally banding it together with E-Z Line

Wire coils can be modeled with curly gray doll hair from a craft store. I did this by untangling loops of the material, then securing it to a styrene false floor in loosely stacked rows with matte medium, **37**.

A very realistic heavy remelt steel scrap load can be made by gluing small broken pieces of models, powdered rust, and bits of shredded silver tinsel over a pre-formed resin scrap load insert (available from Chooch, Motrak, Fine N Scale, and others). Differently colored shapes will greatly improve the three-dimensional appearance of the load, **38**.

Resin and plaster automobile scrap loads sold by many manufacturers can be made more realistic by painting individual details, adding rusty-colored chalk dust, or enclosing a vintage load in an AAR-approved wooden frame, **28**.

1

CHAPTER TWO

Farm machinery and heavy equipment

Farm machinery loads add colorful variety to freight trains in any era. In this view from 1959, a pair of Ford 611 self-propelled combines (built by Oliver Machinery Co., at its Battle Creek, Mich., plant) are blocked and wired down to a 53-foot Chicago & North Western flatcar. The heads are placed on the near end of the car, wired down between pairs of wood stakes.
John Ingles; J. David Ingles collection

Open loads of tractors, combines, bulldozers, scrapers, and other farm and construction equipment are appealing: they simply look cool, and they add variety to the consist of a freight train, **1**. Modeling these open loads and operating them in a manner similar to the prototype is an interesting part of model railroading, and there's a wide variety of potential loads available as commercial plastic and die-cast vehicle models.

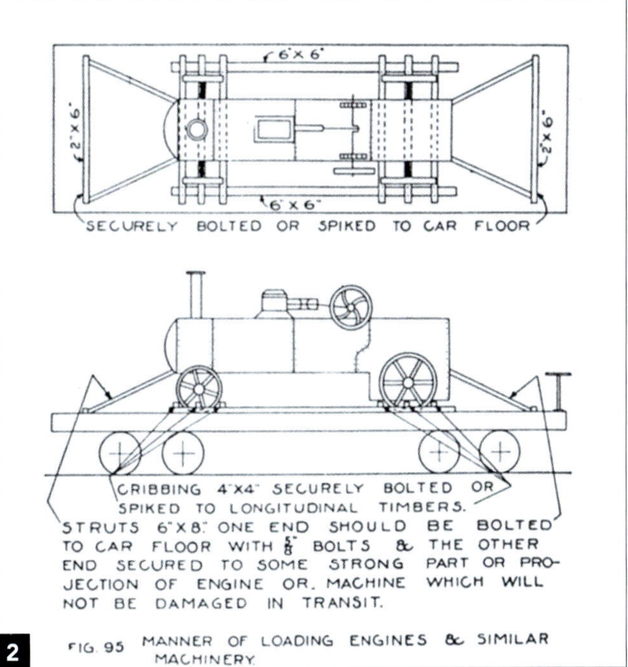

2

Steam tractors were heavy, and they were secured with substantial 4x4, 6x6, and 6x8 wooden timbers around and through the wheels. The cribbing was spiked and bolted together, with the end struts bolted through the floor of the flatcar. This method of securement was replaced by the wire-down method developed by J.I. Case Co. *Keith Kohlmann collection*

3

Workers build a ramp to unload J.I. Case 20-40, 10-20, and 12-25 gas tractors from a Chicago & North Western flatcar spotted on a house track around 1915. *Keith Kohlmann collection*

However, realistically modeling a heavy equipment load is more complex than simply placing a tractor or grader on a flatcar. Equipment varies greatly in size and weight, and many materials and devices have been used to secure these loads to railcars. Also, the methods and materials for doing so have evolved from the steam era through today. So, how do you know what's "right" for what you are modeling?

Uncovering the history of an industry, understanding how it works, how it is served by railroads, and then seeing how it fits with what is already known about railroading can be incredibly satisfying. New gasoline tractors and tractor-drawn equipment streamed out of Allis-

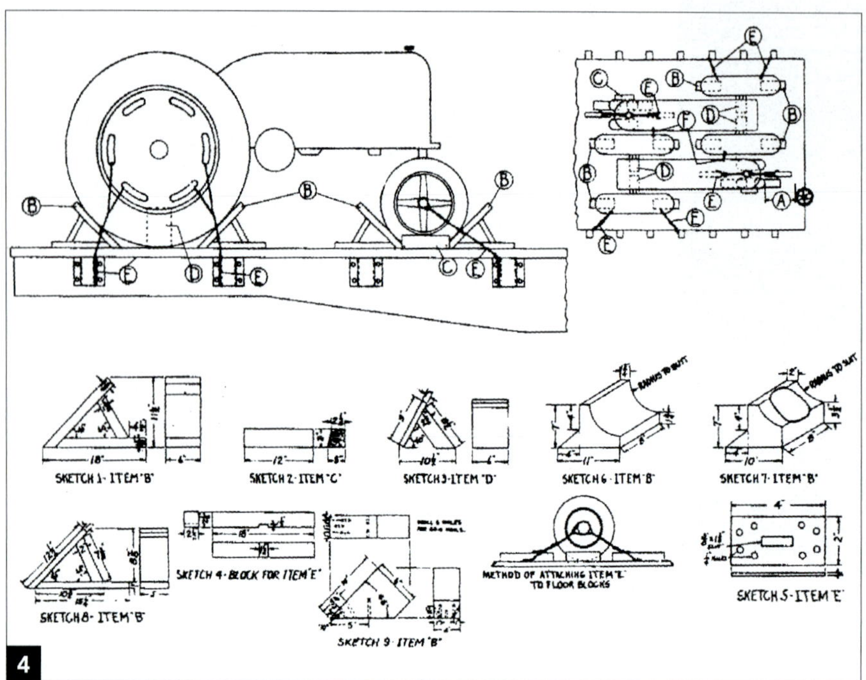

The AAR loading diagram for tractors illustrates the system of wooden blocking with wire tied around the wheels and into the car's stake pockets. *AAR*

Workers tie down a load of Minneapolis-Moline model GT tractors with steel banding at Minneapolis in 1939. This alternative loading practice used rough cut logs for blocking around the tires. Seven 30d nails will be driven into the into the blocks and steel wire will be twisted between the axles and the stake pockets to complete the loading. *Library of Congress*

J.I Case special trains

From 1898 to 1917 the J.I. Case Threshing Machine Company operated special trains each loaded with between 20 and 60 cars of steam engines, threshers, and other harvesting equipment. The goal was to promote newly developed steam-powered farm equipment. This cutting-edge technology was relatively unheard of in many rural communities, and bringing it directly to the people by rail was one of the strategies used by the company. Other farm machinery manufacturers decorated shipments, but only Case operated scheduled promotional trains.

By 1900 Case owned more than 400 custom-built wooden flatcars, 300 of which were 60 feet long with wide decks. The remaining 100 cars were 40-foot heavy-duty truss-rod flatcars designed to carry two steam engines each. At the time, general-service flatcars were narrow and only 36 feet long. Threshing machines are relatively lightweight, and to reach the full weight capacity of 30 tons, a 60-foot car was used. The 60-foot length was also required to set up an operating threshing machine belted to a steam engine on a single car for demonstrations at each stop. The flatcars were painted white with "J.I. Case Threshing Machine Co. Racine, Wis." in big blue letters on the sides.

Case used the cars primarily in the spring and summer. In fall and winter, unused flatcars were leased to the Milwaukee Road. The 60-foot cars were often used to deliver wagons and carriages in the off-season. On one occasion, a large shipment of streetcars from St. Louis Car Co. needed to be moved to California. The Case flatcars were the only available equipment large enough to move them. Because the cars were unusually wide and long, they were restricted to routes with wider clearances (mostly west of Chicago).

At other times, Case sold so much agricultural machinery that the 400 flatcars were in continuous operation. When a large order for a single destination was ready for shipment, it was loaded onto the cars. The entire train from pilot to markers was covered in red,

The J.I. Case Special has just arrived at the Northern Pacific station in Verndale, Minn. on May 28, 1900. The crowd is ready to hear the band and watch a demonstration of the Agitator threshing machine powered by a Case steam tractor, all loaded on a wooden J.I. Case 60-foot flat car. *Racine Heritage Museum Archives*

J.I. Case Threshing Machine Company's

Special Train of 26 Cars

OF

Threshing Machinery

FROM THEIR FACTORY AT

RACINE, WISCONSIN,

TO THEIR BRANCH HOUSE AT

MINNEAPOLIS, MINNESOTA,

In charge of E. L. WRATTEN, Traffic Manager.

VIA

Chicago, Milwaukee & St. Paul Railway

THROUGH

WISCONSIN AND MINNESOTA

By Daylight to Minneapolis as per following Schedule.

This timetable cover from 1900 shows the route of a J.I. Case Special from Racine, Wis., to Minneapolis over the Chicago, Milwaukee & St. Paul. *Keith Kohlmann collection*

white, and blue bunting. Case posters and large banners with the J.I. Case T.M. Co. name and Old Abe logo were attached to the loaded flatcars.

The Case Specials were part of a carefully coordinated advertising campaign. Special train movements were advertised well in advance along the scheduled routes. Posters were put up in each town with the places and times the train would stop. Purchaser's names were also indicated on the posters. The delivery of new machinery was turned into a celebration and used as an opportunity to educate farmers about new products. It gave local dealers an event to attract prospective customers. It was a big attraction to watch the train arrive with new carloads of the latest high-tech farm equipment at the local team track or ramp.

One of the flatcars carried a man dressed up in a red, white, and blue Uncle Sam costume. He played one of the four calliopes that Case sent out on various promotional trains to attract spectators. The calliope was usually located at the center of the train and was powered by a nickel-plated steam engine. The crowd heard speeches from a bandstand built on the last flatcar of the train. Sales and technical representatives met with customers and dignitaries in a Pullman business car at the rear of the train. The sales reps were also members of the brass band that entertained the crowds at each stop. Case advertising buttons were handed out at stops and tossed from the rear platform of the passing train by Uncle Sam.

In the age of horse-powered agriculture, the Case Specials were a high-tech spectacle. They were used effectively to turn ordinary railroad shipments into a much-anticipated event throughout farming communities in the South, West, Midwest, and Great Plains. It was an opportunity to see the machinery, listen to the band and calliope, meet with neighbors, and sometimes take in a motion picture.

At larger cities holding state fairs and agricultural exhibitions, the tractors were unloaded at a ramp near the depot and paraded through the town behind the brass band. The equipment was then driven to the fair for a week of demonstrations. In cities, Case chartered open trolley cars during fair week. The band rode around the city playing and promoting the tractor display.

The Case Specials stopped running in 1917, likely because of rising shipping costs and the need for the replacement of the worn-out flatcars. Also, once the U.S. entered World War I (leading to the formation of the United States Railroad Administration), all special, promotional, and advertising trains were canceled.

Case Specials ran again after 1920, but not as promotional trains. The entire train still carried Case machinery, but it did not include the Case flatcars, band, or calliope. Although they did carry large advertising signs, these trains were strictly for delivering large orders of equipment on railroad-owned flatcars consigned to a single location. These specials were operated occasionally into the early 1960s. Large shipments of Case-New Holland equipment to a single destination can still be seen on the rails today, but they are handled in regular freight trains, and they are not publicized events.

At least 15 loaded flatcars make an impressive sight as they pass through Sherman's Creek, Pa., on June 9, 2012. These export machines were grouped for a single movement, with delivery at a port scheduled to meet a ship headed to Europe. Flatcar OTTX 97771 carries Case IH 8230 and 7130 Axial-Flow combines that are wider than the flatcar. Palletized boxes between the machines carry additional parts. *Keith Kohlmann collection*

This J.I. Case 500 Diesel tractor is waiting outside the Racine, Wis., factory to be shipped to Wilson, Ark., on Dec. 29, 1955. The tractors were loaded diagonally with twisted steel wire tie-downs and wooden blocking. The tractors are equipped with pneumatic rice-field tires.
Racine Heritage Museum Archives

A literal boatload of Allis-Chalmers WD and CA tractors is loaded on the Chesapeake & Ohio car ferry *Badger* at Milwaukee in October 1953. The tractors are loaded crosswise on the flatcars and tied through the frames and blocked on the inside of the tires only.
TRAINS magazine collection

Chalmers, J.I. Case, Caterpillar, and other manufacturing plants at an unprecedented rate during the 1920s. Production of farm equipment took a back seat to military equipment during the World War II era; but production boomed immediately afterward—it took a decade to satisfy the pent-up demand for new and replacement tractors. Demand for construction equipment had been steady, but took off during the Interstate Highway System's rapid construction starting in the 1960s.

A close examination of open equipment loads in each of these eras can provide snapshots of the changing trends in the automotive, manufacturing, and rail industries. This information is fun to learn, and it can deeply influence the work of anyone interested in modeling a particular place or time.

Just as railroad technology continues to evolve, other machine technology is also evolving. The appearance of a particular type of machinery, or even the manufacturers' logos and color schemes, can define a time period on a model railroad in much the same way that the styling of trains, automobiles, signs, and structures defines an era.

For example, a small steel-wheeled tractor can be an appropriate model on a layout through many periods, but it will appear differently depending on which era is being modeled. It would look brand-new in a 1920s setting (working in a field or being delivered on a flatcar); it would likely be weathered and worn sitting next to a barn or in a small field in the 1950s; it could be covered in rust in a patch of tall grass or under an abandoned machine shed on a 1970s-era layout; or it could be freshly painted and restored on display at a museum in the 2000s.

Through the late 1970s flatcars loaded with brightly colored tractors and construction equipment were a common sight in freight trains. Although most of today's new equipment is shipped by trucks, some rail shipment still occurs. Some machines are simply too large for highway travel, and they can only be shipped by rail.

From wood blocks to wire to chains with Trailer Train

From the 1800s into the early 1900s, the railroad industry didn't have a standard set of rules for loading machinery on flatcars. As new technology brought increasingly larger machinery loads to the railroads, it became apparent that a coordinated effort at standardizing loading practices would benefit both railroads and shippers. As an example, steam tractors were secured with heavy 4x4, 6x6, and 6x8 wooden timbers blocked around and through the wheels—an expensive and labor-intensive way to load steam engines, **2**. With their popular special trains (see page 24), the J.I. Case Co. needed to find an alternative to this extensive wooden cribbing around each engine. The company became an essential participant in this phase in the growth of railroad transportation.

Case pioneered many of the methods for moving agricultural machinery by rail in the latter part of the 19th and early 20th centuries. During this period Edward L. Wratten was traffic manager at Case. He coordinated the Case special trains and the delivery of farm equipment on railroads across North America. Railroads worked with Wratten to establish transportation regulations and classifications for the newly emerging

8

Four of 10 Allis-Chalmers WD tractors have been unloaded from this Southern Pacific flatcar at Ithaca, N.Y., on April 16, 1950. The car will be forwarded for a second stop at a distant location, a common method of reducing shipping charges by combining loads for smaller farm equipment dealers. The dunnage hasn't yet been removed; the wires overhanging the side would pose a serious hazard to anyone near the passing car. *Kalmbach Media*

agricultural machinery industry, **3**.

Al Bowman succeeded Wratten as traffic manager at Case. In an interview published in the *Case Factory Eagle* magazine in 1949, Bowman stated, "The wire-down method of securing loads on flatcars, originated at Case many years ago by F.W. Merriman, an outstanding agricultural implement loader, has been copied by other manufacturers and only recently was incorporated in the loading rules of the Association of American Railroads. Using this method, loads are wired to the stake pockets of cars as well as being blocked. Loads have been held in place on flatcars with remarkable success, even in cases of railroad accidents."

This method of securing agricultural machinery was expanded by the AAR to include other types of machinery, including trucks, scrapers, bulldozers, graders, loaders, power shovels, cranes, military equipment, and just about

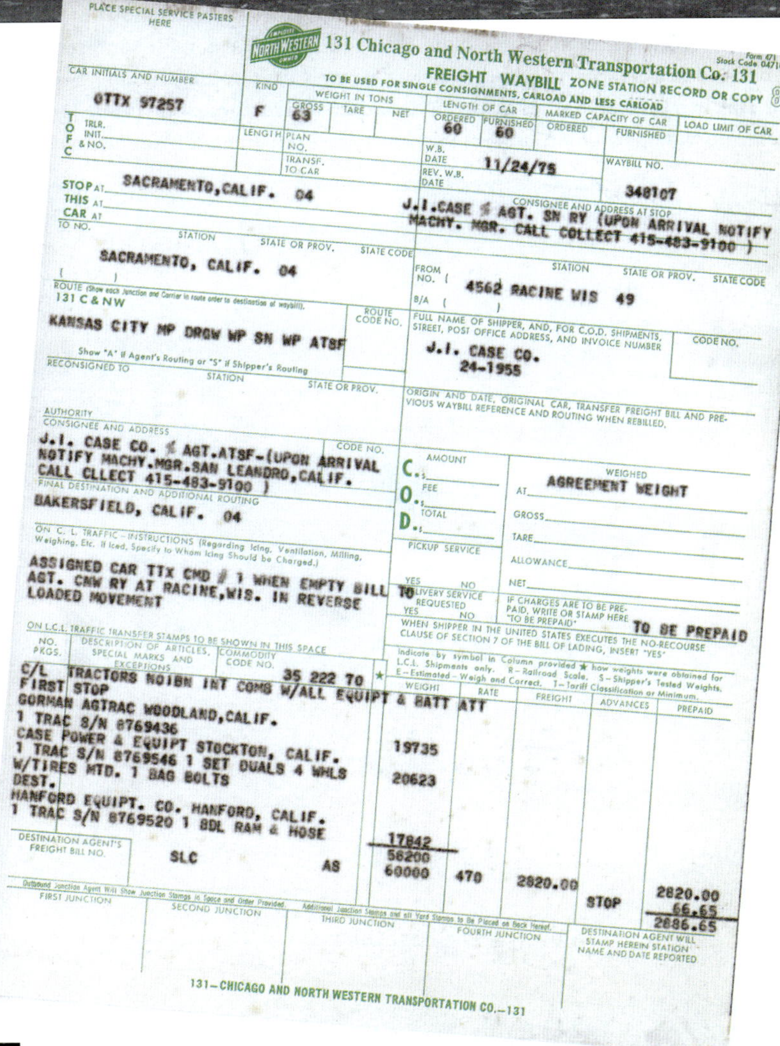

PLACE SPECIAL SERVICE PASTERS HERE

NORTH WESTERN 131 Chicago and North Western Transportation Co. 131
Form 471 Stock Code 04710
FREIGHT WAYBILL ZONE STATION RECORD OR COPY 8
TO BE USED FOR SINGLE CONSIGNMENTS, CARLOAD AND LESS CARLOAD

CAR INITIALS AND NUMBER: OTTX 97257
KIND: F
WEIGHT IN TONS — GROSS: 63 — TARE — NET
LENGTH OF CAR — ORDERED: 60 — FURNISHED: 60
MARKED CAPACITY OF CAR — ORDERED — FURNISHED
LOAD LIMIT OF CAR
TOFC TRLR. INIT. & NO.
LENGTH — PLAN NO. — TRANSF. TO CAR
W.B. DATE: 11/24/75
REV. W.B. DATE
WAYBILL NO.: 348107

STOP THIS CAR AT: SACRAMENTO,CALIF. 04
CONSIGNEE AND ADDRESS AT STOP: J.I.CASE % AGT. SN RY (UPON ARRIVAL NOTIFY MACHY. MGR. CALL COLLECT 415-483-9100)

TO NO. — STATION — STATE OR PROV. — STATE CODE: SACRAMENTO, CALIF. 04
FROM NO. — STATION — STATE OR PROV. — STATE CODE: 4562 RACINE WIS 49
B/A

ROUTE (Show each Junction and Carrier in route order to destination of waybill): 131 C & NW KANSAS CITY MP DRGW WP SN WP ATSF
ROUTE CODE NO.
Show "A" if Agent's Routing or "S" if Shipper's Routing

FULL NAME OF SHIPPER, AND, FOR C.O.D. SHIPMENTS, STREET, POST OFFICE ADDRESS, AND INVOICE NUMBER: J.I. CASE CO. 24-1955
CODE NO.

RECONSIGNED TO — STATION — STATE OR PROV.
ORIGIN AND DATE, ORIGINAL CAR, TRANSFER FREIGHT BILL AND PREVIOUS WAYBILL REFERENCE AND ROUTING WHEN REBILLED.
AUTHORITY

CONSIGNEE AND ADDRESS: J.I. CASE CO. % AGT.ATSF-(UPON ARRIVAL NOTIFY MACHY.MGR.SAN LEANDRO,CALIF. CALL CLLECT 415-483-9100)
CODE NO.
FINAL DESTINATION AND ADDITIONAL ROUTING: BAKERSFIELD, CALIF. 04

C.O.D. AMOUNT $ — FEE $ — TOTAL $
WEIGHED AT: AGREEMENT WEIGHT
GROSS — TARE — ALLOWANCE — NET
PICKUP SERVICE YES NO
DELIVERY SERVICE REQUESTED YES NO

ON C. L. TRAFFIC—INSTRUCTIONS (Regarding Icing, Ventilation, Milling, Weighing, Etc. If Iced, Specify to Whom Icing Should be Charged.)
ASSIGNED CAR TTX CMD # 1 WHEN EMPTY BILL TO AGT. CNW RY AT RACINE,WIS. IN REVERSE LOADED MOVEMENT

IF CHARGES ARE TO BE PREPAID, WRITE OR STAMP HERE "TO BE PREPAID": TO BE PREPAID
WHEN SHIPPER IN THE UNITED STATES EXECUTES THE NO-RECOURSE CLAUSE OF SECTION 7 OF THE BILL OF LADING, INSERT "YES"

ON L.C.L. TRAFFIC TRANSFER STAMPS TO BE SHOWN IN THIS SPACE
Indicate by symbol in Column provided ★ how weights were obtained for L.C.L. Shipments only. R—Railroad Scale. S—Shipper's Tested Weights. E—Estimated—Weigh and Correct. T—Tariff Classification or Minimum.

NO. PKGS.	DESCRIPTION OF ARTICLES, SPECIAL MARKS AND EXCEPTIONS	COMMODITY CODE NO.	★	WEIGHT	RATE	FREIGHT	ADVANCES	PREPAID
C/L	TRACTORS NOIBN INT COMB W/ALL EQUIPT & BATT ATT	35 222 70						
	FIRST STOP							
	GORMAN AGTRAC WOODLAND,CALIF.							
	1 TRAC S/N 8769436							
	CASE POWER & EQUIPT STOCKTON, CALIF.			19735				
	1 TRAC S/N 8769546 1 SET DUALS 4 WHLS W/TIRES MTD. 1 BAG BOLTS			20623				
	DEST.							
	HANFORD EQUIPT. CO. HANFORD, CALIF.							
	1 TRAC S/N 8769520 1 SDL RAM & HOSE			17842				
				58200				
	SLC	AS		60000	470	2820.00		2820.00
							STOP	66.65
								2886.65

DESTINATION AGENT'S FREIGHT BILL NO.

Outbound Junction Agent Will Show Junction Stamps in Space and Order Provided. Additional Junction Stamps and all Yard Stamps to Be Placed on Back Hereof.
FIRST JUNCTION — SECOND JUNCTION — THIRD JUNCTION — FOURTH JUNCTION
DESTINATION AGENT WILL STAMP HEREIN STATION NAME AND DATE REPORTED

131—CHICAGO AND NORTH WESTERN TRANSPORTATION CO.—131

9

A Chicago & North Western freight waybill from Nov. 24, 1975, shows a two-stop load of J.I. Case tractors. The first stop is at Sacramento, Calif., where the car was partially unloaded. Then it was moved to Bakersfield, Calif., for the final unloading. The car, OTTX 97257, is assigned to the C&NW at Racine Junction, Wis., so it is returned empty. *Keith Kohlmann collection*

10

Trailer Train's OTTX no. 92106 is a 60-foot flatcar specifically designed for loading agricultural equipment according to AAR rules. Cars bearing OTTX markings have 64 or 48 3/8" chains with snubbers. Each 8-foot chain is permanently secured to moveable and retractable tie-down winches located in four longitudinal channels that are flush with the wooden deck of the car. This is a typical load of Case 2390 and 2590 tractors circa 1980. The open loading arrangement made the tractors vulnerable to vandalism, and broken windows were a common problem. *Keith Kohlmann collection*

11

Workers load bright yellow Minneapolis-Moline Jet Star 3 tractors using a gantry crane at M-M's Minneapolis plant in 1964. Great Northern no. 64502 is an 89-foot drawbarred machinery flatcar rebuilt from two 42-foot flatcars. Longitudinal channels with winches and chains mounted in the deck and side rails of the car were added to the older flatcars. The tractors can then be secured without the need for wooden blocking. *TRAINS magazine collection*

12

Chicago & North Western 49051 is a 95-foot drawbarred flatcar rebuilt from two obsolete 46-foot flatcars. It's equipped with Brandon tie-downs; two channels built into the floor of the car contain the adjustable tie-downs and chains for securing agricultural tractors and implements. The chains with ratchet tensioning devices can also be locked into the side sill channels for wider loads. Bridge plates span the articulation gap between decks. The load of five J.I. Case 930 Comfort King tractors is considered a single shipment. It's at Dallas in August 1965. *Two photos: Al Chione*

13

Representatives from J.I. Case, Trailer Train, and the Chicago & North Western inspect J.I. Case 1030 Comfort King tractors that have just been ratcheted down onto the deck on a brand new OTTX flatcar outside the factory at Racine, Wis., in September 1966 (left). The car is designed for agriculture loads. At right, conductor George Conrad and crew proudly pose for the Trailer Train photographer after completing a round of "smash testing" the new cars. The crew kicked cuts of loaded flats into standing cars at speeds of 3, 5, 10, and 15 mph. After each collision, the strength of the tie-downs was checked and results analyzed. *Two photos: Keith Kohlmann collection*

any other kind of equipment. More than 100 years later, the wire-down method remains an acceptable method for securing a machinery load; it is still included in AAR rules, **4**.

When pneumatic tires began replacing solid tires on tractors in the 1930s, wooden blocks became an essential way to brace the wheels without damaging the tires. A tire that goes flat while a tractor is in transit could create a shifted load and cause a derailment. Solid blocks of wood and fabricated wedges nailed to the wooden deck of a flatcar became the standard method for blocking wheels with pneumatic tires, **5**. Six strands of No. 9 gauge black annealed wire were wrapped around the axle and threaded through the stake pocket of the flatcar. The wires were then twisted tightly to remove any slack. This technique was repeated at each wheel of every vehicle in the load, **6**.

Depending on their size, tractors could be loaded front to back, diagonally, parallel, or cross-wise in pairs. Shippers tried to place as many tractors on a car without exceeding the load limit, **7**.

Another way shippers reduced charges for smaller shipments was to load a car with tractors for more than one customer. These "two-stop" cars were used primarily with small dealerships that placed small orders, but were more than 400 miles from the manufacturing plant and had rail service (usually a local team track) available, **8**. The car was routed to the first destination on the waybill, **9**, and that dealer removed their portion of the load. The car was then forwarded to the final destination, where the rest of the load was delivered. Partial loads

14

A load of John Deere tractors rides on an OTTX car behind the Union Pacific's Missouri Pacific and Chicago & North Western Heritage Fleet locomotives at Rochelle, Ill., in August 2008. Outside dual rear wheels are strapped to pallets and chained to the deck to keep the load within Plate B clearance limits. *Keith Kohlmann collection*

15

Case New Holland (CNH) tractors are loaded circus-style in the CP Rail yard at Sturtevant, Wis., on Aug. 24, 2012. The ramp was formed from a retired Milwaukee Road flatcar with one truck removed. This group of CNH T8.390 row crop tractors on ITTX flatcars is heading to the Czech Republic via the Port of Philadelphia. *Keith Kohlmann*

A J.I. Case threshing machine has arrived at a siding in Michigan's Upper Peninsula aboard Chicago & North Western flatcar 46963 circa 1907. At remote stations lacking permanent ramps, the standard practice was to construct a temporary ramp from railroad ties for unloading. *Keith Kohlmann collection*

of tractors could be seen arriving in small towns in rural areas through the 1970s. This method of shipping would be interesting to add to the operating scheme of a model railroad.

In 1964 Trailer Train introduced the OTTX 60-foot flatcar, which was specifically designed for transporting agricultural equipment, **10**. These cars had four longitudinal channels flush to the wooden deck. Retractable, moveable Brandon tie-down winches attached to 36 chains, each with snubbers, could be locked into the channels along the outer edges and center of the car.

The railroads' own fleets of older 41-foot and 53-foot flatcars quickly became obsolete. These general-service flatcars required the more time-consuming wire and blocking method of securing loads. The integral ⅜" chains of the OTTX cars were much easier and faster to use. The OTTX cars were also longer, allowing them to carry more equipment than the shorter standard flatcars.

To supplement the OTTX equipment in the Trailer Train pool, many railroads modified groups of their older flatcars with Brandon tie-down equipment. Shorter cars were semi-permanently coupled in pairs with a drawbar. These cars were identified with the same road number with an "A" and "B" suffix, and loads on the combined cars were treated as a single shipment, **11, 12**. Individual railroads also purchased their own 60-foot agricultural equipment cars. Santa Fe, for example, operated a large fleet of cars featuring "Shock Control" cushioned underframes.

In 1966 the J.I. Case Company completed a series of tests on the OTTX flatcars in the yard just outside its plant at Racine Junction, Wis.

This Milwaukee Road flatcar carries part of a large shipment of J.I. Case threshing machines about to leave the Main Works at Racine, Wis., on June 10, 1936. Extensive wooden blocking and twisted wire looped through the wheels secure the load. *Racine Heritage Museum Archives*

An N scale shipment of J.I. Case Baling equipment has been spotted at a freight house dock for unloading. The Athearn car is loaded with modified Wiking balers. Twisted E-Z Line thread and basswood blocks secure the load. *Keith Kohlmann*

Massey-Harris Super Self-Propelled Combines were manufactured in Brantford, Ontario, and shipped by rail across North America. The components of early combines were small enough to fit inside large wooden crates. The self-propelled era meant the end of threshing machines. New York Central 499947 has been temporarily delayed in a derailment at DeKalb, Ill., in 1950, but the load stayed upright and intact. The frames of the crates are bolted to the deck of the car. *Keith Kohlmann collection*

Flatcars loaded with Case tractors were slammed into standing cars at various speeds, and the effects of the collisions were examined, **13**. The OTTX cars passed the tests. The J.I. Case Traffic Department and the Chicago & North Western then set up a dedicated pool of Trailer Train cars assigned to the tractor plant.

The OTTX flatcars with Brandon tie-down equipment have proved to be very reliable, **14**, and they and similar longer cars remain the standard shipping method for agricultural equipment more than 50 years after the initial cars were introduced, **15**.

Threshing machines and harvesting equipment

Threshing machines were the standard method of separating wheat from chaff into the 1940s. The machines are not self-propelled: they operate in a stationary location but are wheeled to enable pulling them from field to field. Threshing machines are relatively lightweight and bulky, **16**, making them a challenge to ship economically. As with tractors, the J.I. Case Co. pioneered the tie-down method of shipping threshers and other harvesting equipment across the continent, **17**. Modelers can copy this method by using Berkshire Junction E-Z Line for all tie-downs. The line is flexible, and it looks like twisted wire. Wrap the line around an axle or glue it with super glue to a tie-down point. Twist the line and glue it in a stake pocket. The lines should be close to a 45-degree angle and symmetrical, **18**.

Shipments of threshing machines

Flatcar OTTX 92056 has delivered a Case IH 2155 Cotton Express cotton picker to a ramp in Texas in May 1997. The plant lifters and other fragile or removable parts were packed inside the basket for shipment. Agricultural equipment is fully set up after it is delivered. *Emery Gulash*

A John Deere 9650 STS Combine on a 60-foot Santa Fe flat passes through Galesburg, Ill., in June 2003. The combine is shipped disassembled with the cutter head, reel, and outside dual wheels chained to the deck. *Dave Nelson*

dropped off quickly after World War II when new self-propelled combines became available (and quickly became popular), **1**. Combines were small at first, and several could be shipped on a single flat car, **19**. Over the years combines grew dramatically in size until by the 1980s a single large machine with its components would typically completely fill a 60-foot flat car, **20**, **21**.

The wooden decks of all the modern agricultural equipment cars allowed shippers the flexibility to nail cleats and blocks into the deck to secure loose parts and secondary equipment. Wires and metal strapping could be secured into stake pockets and side rails, **22**.

An open load of Sperry New Holland round balers has arrived on a team track for unloading at Burlington, Wis., in May 1980. Even with the integral chains and snubbers, this load used wood blocking and straps to secure the load. The Santa Fe flatcar has a Shock Control underframe and is set up to haul farm implements. *Richard Wagner; Keith Kohlmann collection*

23

A Milwaukee Road flatcar carries a new Euclid R-30 off-road haul truck on the Nickel Plate at Euclid, Ohio in 1962. The tires are blocked and the truck is secured to the flatcar with threaded steel rods anchored through the stake pockets. *Trains magazine collection*

This CAT 769D off-highway truck was exported to Spain. The truck was tied down to HTTX 93194 with 12 heavy-duty ½" chains. This is the widest truck that can be shipped by rail without disassembly. It passed through Chicago on May 30, 2007. *Dave Sima*

Construction equipment

In the AAR General Rules for Open Top Loads, Section 3 covers many kinds of construction equipment. The drawings from 1960 illustrate the loading rules for graders, tractors, off-road dump trucks, scarifiers, compactors, dump trailers, and rollers. More drawings were added to the AAR rules over the years as hydraulic cranes and excavators were invented.

Just as the type of automobile can define an era on a layout, so can construction equipment. The Historical Construction Equipment Association (www.hcea.net) has great resources for learning when and where particular machines came into use and what may have replaced them. The website's images of original and restored construction equipment is a great resource for modelers.

How this equipment is loaded and secured is quite similar to tractors and farm machinery. Here's a summary of some of the most common types

25

Wooden blocking around the tires and on the inside of the wheels keeps the load centered on the car. Wood was placed under the pneumatic tires to prevent punctures. The tie-down winches lock into channels set in the floor of the car. Everything is tightened and locked down before this oversize load can be accepted for shipment. *Dave Sima*

26

Caterpillar pull scrapers ride Rock Island flatcars directly behind the locomotives on the Illinois Central around 1959. Open loads of machinery are often placed at the head of the train to minimize slack-action damage. The scraper wheels are held in place with heavy blocking nailed to the wooden flatcar decks. *Trains magazine collection*

27

This N scale model features a Caterpillar No. 80 pull scraper loaded on a Pennsylvania flatcar. The modified Bachmann scraper was painted and lettered with custom decals representing the Caterpillar logo of the mid-1950s, and the flatcar is a customized Walthers model. *Keith Kohlmann*

28

Illinois Terminal no. 1324 is a 60-foot machinery flatcar loaded with a 53-ton Caterpillar 637D scraper near the Peoria, Ill., factory on April 30, 1978. The IT served the plant, and colorful loads of Caterpillar machinery could often be seen loaded on ITC flatcars. *J. David Ingles collection*

29

This Caterpillar scraper load is strong on chains and a bit weak on wooden blocking. The chains with ratchets and snubbers are locked into channels built into the floor of a Progressive Rail flatcar at Sturtevant, Wis., in 2005. The scraper is part of a group of contractor machines being shipped to Pennsylvania for a highway project. *Keith Kohlmann*

30

Santa Fe no. 94414 is a specialty flatcar used for construction and agricultural equipment. A Caterpillar D8K bulldozer equipped with a full cab is at Peoria, Ill., on July 10, 1978. Standard bulldozer blades are about 13 feet wide, so they are shipped detached to avoid oversize load charges and to balance the weight of the load on the flatcar. *J. David Ingles*

Tie-down chains

The advent of specialized flatcars with multiple deck-mounted chains with hooks and ratchets greatly simplified and sped the loading process. This example is from an early 1960s auto-rack car, but similar devices (with varying chain sizes and hook styles) were used on flatcars designed for carrying all types of tractors and construction equipment. The devices can be moved along channels in the deck to the proper locations for each load. The hooks are then connected to the load and the ratchet tightened as needed. *Photo: Santa Fe; James Kinkaid collection*

of equipment, with photos and descriptions showing examples.

Off-highway dump trucks—The 1960 AAR loading diagram for off-highway dump trucks with pneumatic tires calls for heavy wooden blocking nailed to the wooden deck around the wheels, **23**. Threaded steel rods tying the truck to the frame of the flat car were also added by shippers. Trucks' dump beds were locked to prevent the hydraulic bed from lifting while in transit, which would be disastrous when passing under a bridge or entering a tunnel.

Modern off-road dump trucks are shipped on HTTX flat cars with ½" heavy-duty chains locked into the deck channels, **24**. Wooden blocking is still needed around and under the tires. Cable ties are used to keep the ratchet from slipping, **25**.

Scrapers—In the 1920s scrapers (earth movers) transitioned from horse-drawn to tractor-drawn. Scrapers increased in size as the tractors that pulled them also grew. Pull scrapers grew to the maximum width that could

A Caterpillar D9R for export to Japan rides an HTTX flatcar at Galesburg, Ill., on June 28, 2011. The load includes the blade, ripper tooth, and the cab in a crate. *Dave Nelson*

A TTHX car loaded with a Caterpillar D10T bulldozer and another flatcar loaded with a large stationary engine wrapped in plastic have been set out on a side track in a Chicago-area classification yard to avoid being switched over the hump in 2010. The TTHX cars carry heavier (½") chains for loads like these. Wooden blocks keep the chains from scratching the fresh paint. The D10T, with its high drive sprocket, is one of the largest bulldozers that can travel by rail without being disassembled. *Dave Sima*

31

This gondola is carrying part of a multiple-car shipment of Caterpillar export machines going to Japan. The car holds a blade and additional parts for the other machines passing through Galesburg, Ill., in 2011. *Dave Nelson*

This N scale flatcar is a modified Walthers model with a bulldozer from a Bachmann construction vehicle set. The model re-creates a 1955-era Caterpillar D8 bulldozer and additional equipment. Both models have custom decals. The crates are Fine N-Scale parts blocked with basswood. *Keith Kohlmann*

safely travel on a flatcar by the late 1950s, **26**, **27**.

Self-propelled scrapers also followed this path of growth. By the 1960s most major construction equipment manufacturers were producing self-propelled scrapers. These machines grew to be quite heavy and required substantial wooden blocking around the large pneumatic tires, **28**. Special consideration was given to disabling the steering and bowl hydraulics to prevent the joints from moving. Secondary safety cables are looped around the front and back of the scraper for shipment, or ½" chains are used on the ends of a self-propelled scraper, **29**.

Crawler tractors—Bulldozers are produced in sizes that range from small to the Caterpillar D10T, which fills an entire TTHX flatcar. The blade is usually shipped on the same car as the 'dozer, but detached to balance the weight and to keep the load within clearance limits, **30**. Wooden blocking at the ends of the tracks, inside cleats, and outside stub stakes keep the

A pair of Caterpillar 140H graders have arrived on a TTHX car at Cranbrook, B.C., in June 2001. Heavy chains and blocking secure the load to the deck. The blades rest on 2x4 blocks and are chained to keep from rotating. *Keith Kohlmann*

An N scale Hough Payloader is loaded on a Soo Line flatcar (a modified Red Caboose 41-foot flatcar). The Payloader was made from a Wiking Hanomag loader. The body was reshaped, painted, and given custom decals to match a Hough model.
Keith Kohlmann

machines in place. Heavy chains are attached between the stake pockets and the tracks, **31**.

Bulldozer cabs are often shipped in crates attached to the flatcar deck on export loads, **32**. The blades, rippers, support arms, and other attachments are held in place with wooden cleats and chains. Additional parts are shipped loosely chained in gondolas, **33**. A sample model is shown in **34**.

Graders—The AAR requires that pneumatic tires on graders be blocked on all sides, **35**. The heavy blade is rotated to fit entirely on the car, and it is lowered onto blocks and tied with wire or chained in place. Additional wires or chains are placed at 45-degree angles to the load at each corner of the machine.

Loaders—The Hough model HS was the first fully integrated self-propelled wheel loader. Introduced in 1939, the small machine was called a Payloader, and it was designed primarily for unloading bulk material from boxcars. After World War II the Payloaders increased in size and power. They were the primary loader on the market until the late 1950s, **36**. Wheel loaders from various manufacturers continued to grow in size and capacity, **37**. By the late 1960s massive wheel

This TTHX car has just been pulled from the Hough factory in Libertyville, Ill., on June 11, 1972, by the Milwaukee Road switch crew. The load at right is a model 560 Payloader, a 40-ton machine with a 6½-cubic-yard bucket. The company's much-smaller model H-25 Payloader (middle) has a ½-yard bucket. There is about a 15-year difference in technological development between the two designs.
Keith Kohlmann collection

A Clark Equipment Co. Michigan 475B articulated wheel loader fits on a New York Central flatcar at Sharonville, Ohio in April 1973. The bucket and all parts above the driver's compartment have been placed onto the deck so the load can meet clearance limits. The cab, railings, and roll-over protection cover are blocked, nailed, and strapped to the car. The load is as tall as the adjacent boxcar.
Don Dover; Keith Kohlmann collection

Dave Sima used a 1/87 (HO) Tonkin Replicas Caterpillar 972K Wheel Loader and an Intermountain HTTX 60' flatcar to create a very realistic-looking Caterpillar load. [need more details] *Keith Kohlmann*

An HO plastic kit from Kibri was assembled as a replica of a two-car shipment of a Komatsu WA800 Wheel Loader. Dave Sima placed the load on two flatcars to stay within weight limits on the InterMountain flatcars. The wheels and bucket were loaded on MTTX 98102 to meet Plate B clearance. Scale chain and basswood secure the loads. *Keith Kohlmann*

loaders began replacing cable-operated shovels in quarries and construction sites, **38**, as they are faster and more maneuverable, **39**.

Wheel loaders used in surface mining have grown beyond the size of the flatcars used to transport them. The largest loaders are shipped partially assembled. The wheels, bucket, and cab are removed and shipped on an adjacent flatcar to meet clearance requirements, **40**. Loaders can be modified with grapples, bulldozer blades, compaction wheels, and other equipment, **41**. A mine or industry can be defined by the type of specialized equipment that arrives on an inbound open load.

Hydraulic excavators—The type of construction equipment in loads can define an era. Just like multiple types of Trailer Train (TTX) flatcars quickly appeared in the 1960s, the hydraulic excavator followed a similar timeline. These machines quickly replaced cable-operated power shovels. Once established, they became larger and more common, **42**. Hydraulic excavators work in logging, construction, utilities, demolition, mining, and steel industries. With electromagnet and hydraulic shears attachments, they have largely replaced cranes at scrap processing facilities.

Today hydraulic excavators and other construction equipment are manufactured in plants around the world. Various brands can be seen traveling on flatcars. These loads can

A Caterpillar 815F soil compactor is loaded on HTTX 94217 at Galesburg, Ill., in 2004. The wood-deck flatcar was designed for transporting earth-moving equipment. The disassembled frame for a large dump truck is loaded on the next flatcar. *Dave Nelson*

This 56-ton Caterpillar 349E hydraulic excavator is centered on HTTX 80923, balancing the weight between trucks and making this a near-capacity load for the car—placing a heavy load too close to one end will cause axle overloading, even if the overall car weight is within limits. The crawler tracks are chained and blocked, and the dipper arm is chained to prevent it from pivoting or rising while the machine is in transit. It's at Galesburg, Ill., in 2011. *Dave Nelson*

Two Caterpillar 400D articulated dump trucks were loaded onto ITTX 922261 as part of a shipment by Mann Brothers, an excavation contractor, from the CP Rail team track at Sturtevant, Wis., in 2005. The well-used machines are heading to Pennsylvania for a highway project, and it was easier to ship the oversize loads a long distance by rail than on the highway. Used equipment shows rust, mud, and faded paint. *Keith Kohlmann*

be made up of equipment recently imported, manufactured domestically, or headed for export.

Used construction equipment

It's not just new heavy equipment that travels by rail. Contractors use railroads when moving their own heavy equipment to new locations to begin working on new contracts and projects. Moving oversize loads by truck over the Interstate highway system is expensive, time consuming, and labor intensive, which is why many contractors use rail for long-distance moves, **43**.

Used heavy equipment is also moved by rail when it is sold or shipped for repair. Steel-mill rollers and buckets are often seen in open loads around steel mills. Overhead gantry cranes are sent back to the shop for re-conditioning on flatcars. When a mine is closed, useful equipment can be redeployed at distant mines. The machinery is dismantled and shipped to the new location much in the same way that it was initially shipped in. However, the equipment is covered in rust, grease, and dirt.

CHAPTER THREE

Cranes, shovels, and hoists

A rubber-tired American Hoist & Derrick crane rests on a 53-foot Southern Pacific flatcar in April 1960. The tires are blocked on the sides as well as fore and aft. The rear of the body is wired down at each corner, as is the lead wheel, and the boom is blocked and secured to the deck in the down position. *John Ingles; J. David Ingles collection*

The AAR published loading rules for most types of machinery, and a large section of its manual is devoted to cranes and shovels. While most crane loads fit on one or two flatcars, **1**, some of these machines destined for mines were enormous. They were shipped as parts and smaller subassemblies on multiple cars (sometimes dozens or even hundreds).

Regardless of size or manufacturer, these machines followed the same basic construction. A machinery house/cab sits atop a rotating base upon tracks or wheels. A long boom extends outward from the front of the machinery house, with cables allowing the boom to raise/lower, the bucket to open and close (and to control any

A Chesapeake & Ohio carferry offloads two Milwaukee Road 60-foot machinery flatcars loaded with a partially disassembled P&H 670 lattice boom crane at Ludington, Mich., in September 1969. Extensive wood blocking and steel rods through the deck secure the parts. The crawler tracks were removed to maintain clearance. Window glass was covered with heavy cardboard. Notice the overspray of the black paint around the tracks—P&H often did touch-up painting of machinery after loading. *Keith Kohlmann collection*

A small Lorain shovel rides a 53-foot flatcar in the late 1950s (above). It is loaded per the AAR loading diagram (right). The tracks are blocked front and back, threaded steel rods at angles secure the boom just ahead of the cab, and two pairs of threaded rods secure blocks at the front of the boom and atop the bucket to hold it securely to the deck. Not visible at the rear is hardwood cross-bracing wedged beneath the counterweight to prevent damage to the crane and stabilize the load. *Photo: Trains magazine collection; Drawing: AAR*

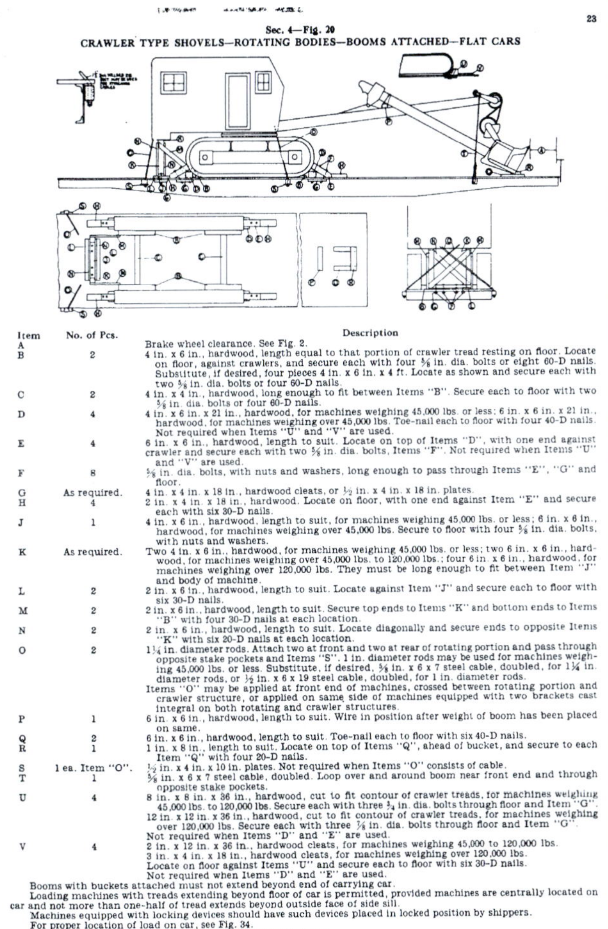

23

Sec. 4—Fig. 20

CRAWLER TYPE SHOVELS—ROTATING BODIES—BOOMS ATTACHED—FLAT CARS

Item	No. of Pcs.	Description
A		Brake wheel clearance. See Fig. 2.
B	2	4 in. x 6 in., hardwood, length equal to that portion of crawler tread resting on floor. Locate on floor, against crawlers, and secure each with four ⅝ in. dia. bolts or eight 60-D nails. Subsitute, if desired, four pieces 4 in. x 6 in. x 4 ft. Locate as shown and secure each with two ⅝ in. dia. bolts or four 60-D nails.
C	2	4 in. x 4 in., hardwood, long enough to fit between Items "B". Secure each to floor with two ⅝ in. dia. bolts or four 60-D nails.
D	4	4 in. x 6 in. x 21 in., hardwood, for machines weighing 45,000 lbs. or less; 6 in. x 6 in. x 21 in., hardwood, for machines weighing over 45,000 lbs. Toe-nail each to floor with four 40-D nails. Not required when Items "U" and "V" are used.
E	4	6 in. x 6 in., hardwood, length to suit. Locate on top of Items "D", with one end against crawler and secure each with two ⅝ in. dia. bolts, Items "F". Not required when Items "U" and "V" are used.
F	8	⅝ in. dia. bolts, with nuts and washers, long enough to pass through Items "E", "G" and floor.
G	As required.	4 in. x 4 in. x 18 in., hardwood cleats, or ½ in. x 4 in. x 18 in. plates.
H	4	2 in. x 4 in. x 18 in., hardwood. Locate on floor, with one end against Item "E" and secure each with six 30-D nails.
J	1	4 in. x 6 in., hardwood, length to suit, for machines weighing 45,000 lbs. or less; 6 in. x 6 in., hardwood, for machines weighing over 45,000 lbs. Secure to floor with four ⅝ in. dia. bolts, with nuts and washers.
K	As required.	Two 4 in. x 6 in., hardwood, for machines weighing 45,000 lbs. or less; two 6 in. x 6 in., hardwood, for machines weighing over 45,000 lbs. to 120,000 lbs.; four 6 in. x 6 in., hardwood, for machines weighing over 120,000 lbs. They must be long enough to fit between Item "J" and body of machine.
L	2	2 in. x 6 in., hardwood, length to suit. Locate against Item "J" and secure each to floor with six 30-D nails.
M	2	2 in. x 6 in., hardwood, length to suit. Secure top ends to Items "K" and bottom ends to Items "B" with four 30-D nails at each location.
N	2	2 in. x 6 in., hardwood, length to suit. Locate diagonally and secure ends to opposite Items "K" with six 20-D nails at each location.
O	2	1¼ in. diameter rods. Attach two at front and two at rear of rotating portion and pass through opposite stake pockets and Items "S". 1 in. diameter rods may be used for machines weighing 45,000 lbs. or less. Substitute, if desired, ⅝ in. x 6 x 7 steel cable, doubled, for 1¼ in. diameter rods, or ½ in. x 6 x 19 steel cable, doubled, for 1 in. diameter rods. Items "O" may be applied at front end of machines, crossed between rotating portion and crawler structure, or applied on same side of machines equipped with two brackets cast integral on both rotating and crawler structures.
P	1	6 in. x 6 in., hardwood, length to suit. Wire in position after weight of boom has been placed on same.
Q	2	6 in. x 6 in., hardwood, length to suit. Toe-nail each to floor with six 40-D nails.
R	1	1 in. x 8 in., length to suit. Locate on top of Items "Q", ahead of bucket, and secure to each Item "Q" with four 20-D nails.
S	1 ea. Item "O".	½ in. x 4 in. x 10 in. plates. Not required when Items "O" consists of cable.
T	1	⅝ in. x 6 x 7 steel cable, doubled. Loop over and around boom near front end and through opposite stake pockets.
U	4	8 in. x 8 in. x 36 in., hardwood, cut to fit contour of crawler treads, for machines weighing 45,000 lbs. to 120,000 lbs. Secure each with three ¾ in. dia. bolts through floor and Item "G". 12 in. x 12 in. x 36 in., hardwood, cut to fit contour of crawler treads, for machines weighing over 120,000 lbs. Secure each with three ⅞ in. dia. bolts through floor and Item "G". Not required when Items "D" and "E" are used.
V	4	2 in. x 12 in. x 36 in., hardwood cleats, for machines weighing 45,000 to 120,000 lbs. 3 in. x 4 in. x 18 in., hardwood cleats, for machines weighing over 120,000 lbs. Locate on floor against Items "U" and secure each to floor with six 30-D nails. Not required when Items "D" and "E" are used.

Booms with buckets attached must not extend beyond end of carrying car.

Loading machines with treads extending beyond floor of car is permitted, provided machines are centrally located on car and not more than one-half of tread extends beyond outside face of side sill.

Machines equipped with locking devices should have such devices placed in locked position by shippers.

For proper location of load on car, see Fig. 34.

See General Rules 4, 5, 9, 14, 15, 19 and 19A for further details.

Not even a serious derailment could break this Link-Belt Speedcrane (right) or John Deere tractors (left) free from their flatcars, demonstrating that the wooden blocking and twisted wire method of securing machinery loads was very effective. This provides a good view of the blocking under the rear of the Link-Belt machinery house, which locked the turntable in place. This wreck was on the Chicago Great Western at Lombard, Ill., on June 1, 1948.
Cole Collection, Lake States Railway Historical Association

other boom attachments, such as a hook or electromagnet). The machinery house pivots upon the base to turn the boom.

The back of a crane or shovel machinery house contains counterweights, which balance the weight of the boom on the front. On larger machines, these counterweights are shipped detached from the machinery house to stay within width and weight restrictions. Shippers must take care to balance crane loads evenly on the flatcar. Crane booms for larger cranes are shipped in sections stacked on a flatcar. Crawler tracks are allowed to hang over the side of the car, but only if at least half of each track width is in contact with the deck of the car. Wider crawler tracks are shipped detached from the truck side frame. Buckets, shovels, attachments, and cabs can also make up the two or three flatcar loads needed to ship the largest construction cranes and shovels, **2**.

Small shovels and cranes are shipped nearly completely assembled with symmetrical tie-down cables placed at 45-degree angles, **1**, **3**. Booms are blocked with hardwood and rest on the deck of the flatcar. Crawler tracks are blocked along the inboard sides and on the ends. Three or more wooden stub stakes prevent lateral movement of the shovel.

The most critical movement to prevent is the bouncing or rotation of the machinery house. Heavy hardwood timber bracing is placed under the counterweight to keep the house from bouncing and destroying the turntable mechanism, **4**. The house must be secured to prevent any rotation that might cause to boom to fall off the car or strike lineside objects, **5**, **6**.

5

A Bucyrus-Erie 22-B crane leaves the plant in Erie, Pa., in July 1958. The crane is secured with wooden blocks and cables. The crane boom is blocked, and the lines are slack. The load on the Seaboard Air Line flatcar includes a backhoe boom. Smaller construction cranes and shovels were manufactured at B-E's Erie plant.
Bob's Photos

This N scale Northwest shovel load is handled right behind the locomotives for the long trip from Green Bay, Wis., to a quarry in Metalline Falls, Wash. The model started with a metal kit from Langley that was modified with styrene to match the Brooks Stevens styling of the prototype. The heavy load was balanced on a Micro-Trains flatcar, similar to the way it would have been loaded at the factory, with stripwood blocking at the rear of the cabin and on the crawler tracks. Non-fraying rayon thread and custom decals complete the mid-1950s-era models. *Keith Kohlmann*

Bucyrus-Erie open loads

The Marion Power Shovel Company and Bucyrus-Erie built the world's largest stripping shovels. Beginning with the original steam-powered railroad shovels, mining equipment grew at an astonishing rate through the 20th century, **7**. Electric shovels replaced steam shovels in the 1920s, and the two companies competed for the "World's Largest Shovel" title over the next five decades.

Both companies manufactured steam shovels, draglines, blast hole drills, and power shovels. The machines were built in subassemblies that were shipped by rail to the mine site for final assembly, **8**. This was the only feasible way to produce these machines, making transportation a critical part of the assembly process. Each step was carefully planned, and shipments of machinery could range from two carloads for a blast hole drill, **9**, to 300 cars for a huge stripping shovel.

In October 1962 the Bucyrus-Erie 3850-B stripping shovel "River King" was completed for Peabody Coal Company for its open-pit mine near

This flatcar carries one of four crawler truck frames that will form the base of "Big Brutus," an 11-million-pound Bucyrus-Erie 1850-B electric stripping shovel. The truck frames were among the first parts to be shipped from the B-E plant in South Milwaukee, Wis., to a Pittsburg & Midway Coal Co. mine near Hallowell, Kan., on Aug. 4, 1961. The shovel required 150 railcars to ship and more than a year to assemble. The 115,470-pound crawler truck frame rests on 4x6 hardwood blocks. The ends are braced with 6x12 timbers secured with threaded steel rods running through the deck of the flat car. The crawler frame is tied down with steel cables threaded through hooks placed in the stake pockets. *Keith Kohlmann collection*

This flatcar is loaded with two electric drive motors and the nested halves of the machinery house for a Bucyrus-Erie 190-B electric shovel. The motors are bolted to the deck, while the house is supported on steel brackets and banding. The car is part of a multi-car shipment ready to leave the factory at South Milwaukee for Minnesota's Iron Range in 1952. *Keith Kohlmann collection*

A Bucyrus-Erie 40-R blast hole drill is ready for shipment from South Milwaukee in 1955. The boom is braced by a wooden frame and the drill rests on hardwood blocking. The windows are covered with boards and loose parts are in a crate. Heavy cables tie the drill to the stake pockets. The wide crawler tracks and additional parts are shipped on a separate flatcar. *Keith Kohlmann collection*

Lenzburg, Ill., 30 miles southeast of East St. Louis, Ill. It took 300 carloads to ship the shovel to the mine, **10**. The "River King" was the largest shovel ever built by B-E, and at the time it was the largest mobile land machine in the world. With a boom 200 feet high, the stripping shovel could scoop 140 cubic yards (220 tons) of overburden, drop it 464 feet away, then swing back its boom at a speed of 25 mph for the next bite in just 50 seconds. In one day, this 18-million-pound machine could dig the tonnage hauled by 1,700 railroad cars. These massive coal-stripping shovels permanently transformed the coal mining industry (and the environment) throughout the region.

Bucyrus International (now Caterpillar) still produces some of the largest mining shovels and draglines in the world. Custom-production draglines can weigh more than 16 million pounds. They operate with a 360-foot boom, lifting 150 to 200 tons of overburden with each bite.

These excavators must be shipped out of the plant in pieces and assembled at the mining sites. On just about any given day, flatcars and gondolas can be seen loaded with huge boom segments, **11**, crawler frames, buckets, motors, electrical, and hoisting gear waiting for pickup outside the plant, **12**. A modern blast-hole drill leaves the plant as a single shipment on two or three flatcars.

On new equipment, the booms and crawler frames are painted gloss black; a large "Bucyrus" nameplate with white letters is mounted just below the boom-point sheaves, **13**. Booms painted in the old scheme were olive green with the entwined Bucyrus-Erie logo. The machinery house was usually golden yellow and maroon. Some mine owners specified machines in their corporate colors. Until recently, machines often left the plant painted in red primer, but now they are primed light gray, then finished in the color scheme specified by the mine owner after assembly in the field. Blast-hole

The upper and lower halves of the front face of a 115-yard dipper are secured inside an Elgin, Joliet & Eastern gondola with cables and wooden blocking. The car is one of 300 required to ship Bucyrus-Erie's 3850-B "Big Hog" shovel to Peabody Coal Company's Sinclair Mine in western Kentucky on May 12, 1962. *Keith Kohlmann collection*

11

Wooden beams and threaded steel rods support the boom of a Bucyrus-Erie 190-B shovel on Chicago, Burlington & Quincy flatcar no. 94692. Cables wrapped around the upper arms of the boom are secured into stake pockets. Idler cars on either end don't contact the main load, but they carry additional parts for the shovel. It's at the South Milwaukee plant on July 12, 1960. *Keith Kohlmann collection*

drills were painted maroon and golden yellow in the 1950s, and today are usually painted white or Cat yellow.

The huge subassemblies are designed in standardized units that fit railroad clearances. Each piece of a machine must meet rail clearances not only on the North American route they'll be taking, but also in the country to which it will be heading. The loads make the first leg of their journey by rail. About 75 percent of these machines are headed to international ports where the parts are transloaded onto ships. Some of these loads only travel 7.5 miles north by rail to the Port of Milwaukee where one of the largest heavy lift cranes on the Great Lakes is available for hoisting these parts onto ships; others head to ports on a coast. International destinations for the machines include surface mines in Australia, Peru, South Africa, and China.

Components heading to North American mines travel by rail, like a recent shipment of seven 2.4 million-pound shovels to a tar sands project north of Fort McMurray, Alberta, or mining shovels shipped by rail to coal mines in Wyoming's Powder River Basin or surface mines in Colorado and New Mexico. For more than a century, Bucyrus shovels, draglines, and drills have been shipped to the bituminous coal fields of Southern Illinois, Indiana, Kentucky, Kansas, and Oklahoma, to phosphate mines in Florida, iron mines in Minnesota and Quebec, stone quarries in California, and copper mines in Montana. Bucyrus machinery has been shipped to 161 nations worldwide, **14**.

Heavy components are secured with thick threaded-steel rods bolted or welded directly through the frame of the flatcar or the sides of a gondola, **15**. Parts are also anchored through stake pockets of flatcars or with angle-iron fixtures welded to the steel deck. Smaller parts are held in place with steel strapping, and many loads are secured with wire rope. Sensitive and fragile components are enclosed in wooden crates. Wood blocking is placed around and beneath the parts to minimize any damage that might occur

12

A Louisville & Nashville flatcar is loaded with three dragline buckets at South Milwaukee in June 1956. Extensive blocking, banding, and cables secure the loads. The flatcar in the foreground is loaded with 5-, 6-, and 12-cubic-yard dragline buckets. It is coupled to a separate flatcar carrying a 30-yard dragline bucket resting on its side. In the background is a loaded 40-R blast hole drill. The drill's wide crawler tracks have been loaded on a separate flatcar to meet railroad clearances. *Keith Kohlmann collection*

The boom for a Bucyrus-Erie 295-B electric rope shovel leaves the factory on an OTTX flatcar in 1973. Heavy wooden cribbing, stub stakes, and steel rods anchor the 50-foot boom. *Keith Kohlmann collection*

Union Pacific flatcar no. 58893 carries a large dipper bucket and two hoisting sheaves at the Bucyrus-Erie plant in Pocatello, Idaho, in April 1977. Threaded-steel rods tie the bucket and wooden blocking to the flatcar. *Keith Kohlmann collection*

This QTTX flat is loaded with a 14-foot-tall truck frame that will support the rotating machinery house of a Bucyrus 495HR/LGI electric rope shovel. The frame is loaded on its side for the trip to a Wyoming coal mine (top). The photo above illustrates the use of threaded steel rods and angle iron welded to the deck to secure the 191,430-pound frame. Very little wooden blocking is required. The car was assigned to the Bucyrus plant in South Milwaukee in 2004.
Two photos: Keith Kohlmann

if the load shifts or vibrates during transit. Wood is also strapped over unpainted machined areas to protect bearing surfaces and maintain critical tolerances. If there is room on the flatcar deck, lighter loads are filled out with miscellaneous parts like enormous cast-steel track links.

Some of the loads, particularly the boom sections, are longer than an 89-foot flatcar. Empty idler flatcars are positioned beneath the overhanging portions of large parts that are longer than the car on which they are loaded. These idler flats do not contact the load. Excess-height parts travel on depressed-center flatcars, while extremely heavy castings and assemblies are shipped on heavy-duty flatcars of up to 250-ton capacity. When several heavily loaded cars leave the plant together, they are placed between other less-heavily loaded cars to more evenly distribute the load on bridges and the track structure. Empty cars are also cut in between loads to provide increased braking capability in short trains.

Generations of railfans have enjoyed watching the fascinating outbound loads leave the Milwaukee-area plant. A friend related that in 1969 he saw a brand new Chicago & North Western SD45 with a caboose and crew waiting outside the plant on the interchange track. He struck up a conversation with the conductor, who said they were running as a special movement. They were waiting for a hot load to come out of the plant. The train was running on the C&NW as far south as St. Louis, and it was not to be delayed. The part had to meet a ship leaving New Orleans for South America later that week.

Railfans regularly stop near the Rawson Avenue crossing to watch the Bucyrus crew quickly and efficiently switch the shop buildings. There is always a sense of anticipation as one waits to see what kind of impressive flatcar load might be pulled out of one of the mammoth shop buildings, **16**. Stenciling on the parts will often reveal the mine or country to which the machine is heading.

Many modelers use prototype

The Bucyrus plant switcher, a GE 44-tonner, eases a Union Pacific gondola to the welding shop at South Milwaukee in August 2018. The gondola is loaded with the counterweight box for the back of a 495 shovel. *Keith Kohlmann*

An N scale switcher slowly passes the interchange tracks outside the Bucyrus-Erie plant in 1956. The SW9 is a Life-Like model and the boom and bucket loads are modified from parts of an HO scale power shovel made by Boley. Basswood blocking and rayon thread secure the loads to the Micro-Trains flatcars. *Keith Kohlmann*

photos to build accurate and dramatic open loads, **17**. As with other construction equipment, there are many models of cranes and shovels that can be used as loads. Copy what you see in prototype photos for loading, blocking, and tie downs to achieve the most realistic loads.

The smaller parts for most of today's big shovels coming from Bucyrus (now Caterpillar) and P&H (now Komatsu Mining) are shipped to mines for assembly on flatbed trucks or in standard shipping containers from global suppliers. But the truck frame, crawler side frames, boom, and counterweight box are too big to ship by truck, so these shovel parts are still moved by rail.

Marion and Bucyrus are now merged, and under the Caterpillar name. Shovels are not as large today, but they are still far too big to ship assembled. Railroads offer the only clearances large enough to ship the biggest shovel parts over land.

CHAPTER FOUR

Vessels, transformers, and oversize loads

A special movement of an Air Products coil-wound LNG heat exchanger travels behind CSX SD60I no. 8734 at West Trenton, N.J., in May 2003. The heat exchanger is approximately 15 feet in diameter, 180 feet long, and weighs 200 tons. It travels on two heavy-duty flatcars with two idlers. Crew members ride in a caboose while watching the load. *Keith Kohlmann collection*

Miscellaneous bulky items make up a large share of open loads, including tanks, **1**, boilers, generators, **2**, turbines, transformers, circuit breakers, refinery components, reactor vessels, wind generator components, various machine and factory parts, and random items too numerous to list. Many are oversize and overweight, requiring special handling.

Allis-Chalmers built this generator at West Allis, Wis. It's loaded aboard a six-axle, two-truck New York Central depressed-center flat bound for a power plant in Dixon, Ill. It will travel in a special movement limited to 15 mph; the wide load means no meets with opposing trains or cars on passing sidings are allowed en route. Threaded steel rods secure the 185-ton load. *Chicago & North Western*

How these items are handled and loaded depends upon their size and weight. Many ride on standard flatcars or gondolas, and others require heavy-duty or specialized cars. In general, standard cars are used if possible; using a longer or higher-capacity car than required by the load adds expense to the shipment.

Depressed-center and heavy-duty flatcars

Oversize loads often travel on depressed-center flatcars. The deck of a conventional flatcar is about 4'-6" above the rails, **3**. Depressed-center flatcars have a center deck that drops down 2 feet lower than the end decks located above the trucks. This places the load closer to the rails, allowing the car to carry taller dimensional loads. The depressed center also lowers the center of gravity of the load. The bottom of the frame can ride as low

A large cylindrical-shaped machine component has a custom-built wooden cradle made from timbers and wedges bolted to the deck of a Southern flatcar. Steel rods with turnbuckles secure the load tightly in place. The load passed through Racine, Wis., in July 1978. *Richard Wagner; Keith Kohlmann collection*

A tall pressure-vessel load is bolted to the deck of a depressed-center flatcar and secured with threaded steel rods. It's about to depart the BNSF yard at Cicero, Ill., in January 2009. *Dave Sima*

An Allis-Chalmers heavy-duty 12-axle, 4-truck flatcar (ACMX 403) rolls through Rondout, Ill., in May 1979 with a heavy load wrapped in plastic, bolted to steel I-beams, and braced by 12 steel rods. *Keith Kohlmann collection*

as 2.5" above the rail, **4**. Historically, most Class 1 railroads have maintained small fleets of depressed-center flatcars (AAR class FD) on their rosters.

Depressed-center flats vary widely in size, capacity, and construction. They represent a wide range of specialty equipment designed to carry excess-height (and excess-weight) loads. Many are designed to carry very heavy loads, some up to 450 tons, but not all depressed center flatcars are built for carrying heavy loads. The load capacity range begins at 75 tons and increases as the size of the frame and the number of axles increases. Depressed-center flatcars can have 4, 8, 12, 16, or 20 axles with multiple four- or six-wheel trucks. The ends of many of these cars ride on span bolsters that spread the weight over multiple trucks, **5**.

The load limit of a car depends on the strength of the car frame, the number of axles, the type of trucks, and how the length of the car distributes the weight of the load over a certain distance. Extremely heavy loads, or loads that are more concentrated near the center of the car, require a stronger frame and a longer wheelbase. This spreads the load over a wider area and reduces the forces directed into bridges and the track structure. The force of a concentrated load must be distributed to keep it from bending or breaking the flatcar, **6**.

As specialized equipment, depressed-center flatcars are generally not used to carry a load that would ship comfortably on a flat-deck car; likewise, heavy-duty cars are not used to carry loads that are well below their weight capacity. Many of these

The idler cars that were placed between loads of fractioning tower sections have been removed, and welders have begun to cut through the support rods holding the tower sections in place. Steel supports were welded between the load and the bracing on QTTX 131042, an example of a heavy-duty straight-deck, eight-axle flatcar. This very heavy open load arrived at Newport, Minn., in the mid-1990s. *Bob Gallegos*

specialty cars are assigned to a shipper or move among a group of shippers in a tightly scheduled manner.

The frames are made from a large single casting or welded construction. On older cars the end decks were often covered with wood planks, while the center deck was covered by steel plate. The wood decking allowed for large spikes to be nailed into the end decks to secure blocking, **7**.

In the steam era, holes were sometimes drilled or burned (cut by torch) into the decks of cars to allow steel rods to pass through the deck, with the ends of the rods secured below the floor with steel plates. However, this practice is strictly prohibited today. Drilling through—or welding supports onto—the cast sections of the flatcar is not allowed because it compromises the structural strength of the deck. Welding is also prohibited in the curved transition area between the upper and lower decks unless a shear block pad is part of the car specifically for providing a place to safely weld to the car. Modern cars have these locations clearly marked. Steel end stops and load supports can only be welded to the steel decks.

This Allis-Chalmers electrical transformer is mounted on Chicago & North Western depressed-center flat no. 48009 using heavy wooden timbers and threaded steel rods. This unusual use of wood bracing may have been caused by a nationwide steel shortage. The car is at Milwaukee in September 1951. *Linn Wescott*

All securements and dunnage must be removed by the current shipper or consignee before the empty car is returned. The decks of these cars show the welding scars of securements from previous loads. Some cars in dedicated service to a particular shipper retain their securements when traveling empty back to the plant for another load. Cars may also have a system of permanent holes in the deck for securing risers, bunks, and other attachment devices used to secure loads.

Most of today's depressed-center flatcars are operated by TTX or Kasgro Rail. These cars are primarily used for heavy machinery and other industrial components that are too large or too heavy to move on a highway. The shipments originate primarily from the power generation and energy industries, with the most common loads being electrical transformers, tanks and pressure vessels, boilers, turbines, wind-energy hubs and nacelles, and oversized components from mining shovels and dump trucks.

Operation and handling

With oversize/overweight loads, consulting with shippers, scheduling the cars for loading, planning the routing, then moving the loads is a complicated process, **8**. Railroads maintain specialized departments to serve customers by coordinating shipments that require specialized equipment, special handling, or train operation, **1**. Multiple cars with extra heavy and oversized loads are often collected together to travel as a special movement. In the case of export loads, a manufacturer might load and hold several cars until an entire multi-car shipment is complete. Then the movement is scheduled to arrive just in time to meet a ship at an ocean port.

Special loads are placed at the head of a freight train to minimize shocks to the loads while traveling. Trains handling these special loads operate under restricted speeds (usually 25 to 45 mph) to reduce damage to the loads, track, and bridges. Special loads receive extra attention in classification yards. They are sorted by flat switching, rather than being rolled over a hump as with other cars. Special cars are placed on a separate track in classification yards where they will not be slammed into by other cars coming off the hump. These cars are marked with signs saying "Do Not Hump"—this is also noted in the conductor's reports.

8

This 500-ton nuclear reactor required a special move as its own train on the Milwaukee Road in 1977, including idler cars and two cabooses for crew members. To clear the high/wide load, lineside signals and other near-track obstructions had to be removed and track shifted under some bridges; no trains or cars could be on the parallel mainline track. The 49-mile trip from Savanna, Ill., to Byron, Ill., took eight hours. *David Franzen*

9

A switch crew was called for Chicago & North Western Extra 1069 East to make a special movement of a very large Allis-Chalmers transformer that needed to make a connection in Chicago. The N scale scene features a modified Atlas flatcar. The load is made from the eyepiece of a Kodak 110 pocket camera, braced with styrene strips and E-Z Line. Special rail movements can add interest to operating sessions. *Keith Kohlmann*

10

Large hardwood timbers support this heavy turbine load on a heavy-duty, straight-deck Delaware & Hudson flatcar at Binghamton, N.Y., in January 1988. The beams are bolted to the car, and steel angle iron welded to the deck braces the wooden assembly. The bearing surface of the turbine is wrapped with a protective layer of plastic.
Keith Kohlmann collection

A boy looks up at a massive Westinghouse generator riding on a multi-truck car in 1971. The Santa Fe took this publicity photo as it carried the 650-ton load on the last leg of its journey from East Pittsburgh to Oklahoma Gas & Electric at Konawa, Okla. *Santa Fe*

The routes of special cars are planned to ensure that high, wide, or very heavy loads can clear narrow places like tunnels or bridges and ride safely on well-maintained track. Particularly urgent, valuable, or sensitive loads might make up the consist of an entire train movement, even if it is only a single car, **9**. In the case of extremely heavy loads, additional empty freight cars (idler cars) are often placed between the loaded cars to distribute the weight and give the train additional braking capacity.

Some extremely high and wide loads require specialized handling. They are placed in a train dedicated to moving only that load. These trains often include a caboose for a crew to coordinate movements with the railroad. They monitor the load while in transit. Fracking towers are one type of load that is manufactured in a factory, then shipped to oil refineries and LNG plants in special trains. Oversize loads sometimes require modifying bridges or lineside structures (signals, pole lines, relay cases) to clear the load.

Some or all of these speed, clearance, and handling restrictions can be added to an operating session to create interest and challenges. If an industry

A 50-foot vacuum dehydrator is ready to leave the Rex Chain Belt factory in Milwaukee aboard a New York Central flatcar in July 1959. The dehydrator is consigned to a Lipton Tea plant at Suffolk, Va. The load is bolted to the deck of the car and wrapped by steel rods and banding. *Keith Kohlmann collection*

13

Angle iron has been welded to the deck of this Canadian Pacific depressed-center flatcar to hold a large transformer in place. Large bolts and steel rods secure the load. Palletized radiators are nailed and strapped to the upper decks. It's at Cleburne, Texas, in March 1986. *K.B. King, Jr.; Lloyd Keyser collection*

regularly ships oversized or heavy loads, then the scheduled movement of a dedicated set of equipment can be a regular part of operations.

Heavy-duty flatcars are often used to move parts used in the production of energy where economies of scale are gained by building the machinery as big as possible, **10**. Due to clearance and weight constraints, massive generators, **11**, turbines, boilers, fracking towers, windmills, electrical transformers, and mill and factory equipment, **12**, can only be transported by rail on specialized flatcars. Engineers designing this equipment must pay close attention to how it will be shipped to its final destination, **13**, **14**, **15**. Railroads have been rebuilding their infrastructure to meet the changing weight and clearance needs of shippers for more than a century, **16**.

From mining trucks to parts for rockets, **17**, and the Space Shuttle, **18**, very large parts are designed to be shipped by rail. The limitation of rail clearance is a consideration in much of the technological machinery all around us. However, these limitations do not stop production.

14

A spherical gas holder rests on wooden blocks and is braced with steel rods to keep it stable on its flatcar in July 1969. The loading plan for unusual loads must be approved before the car can be moved. *Keith Kohlmann collection*

This stator core (part of a generator) and mounting equipment weighs 185 tons, requiring a heavy-duty four-truck flatcar. The core was built in England and is being transloaded from a ship at Sorel, Quebec, in the late 1950s. It's 12 feet wide and 13 feet tall. It traveled to Toronto as a special movement, a four-day trip with a 10-mph speed limit. *Canadian National*

Allis-Chalmers

Allis-Chalmers manufactured massive electrical generating and mill equipment at its West Allis (Wis.) Works. Transformers, steam and hydroelectric turbines, condensers, stone crushers, and kilns were all shipped by rail from the sprawling complex. The plant contained 21 miles of track and had three switching locomotives, **19**. Like competitors General Electric and Westinghouse, Allis-Chalmers shipped transformers weighing more than 200 tons on eight-axle depressed-center flatcars. Both the Milwaukee Road and the Chicago & North Western served the plant. Depressed-center and heavy-duty flatcars were provided by these railroads.

The company also owned a small fleet of well cars (painted in company's Persian Orange color scheme) for moving one-piece ring bearings for mill equipment, gears, and oversized condensers for nuclear power plants (an O gauge model of this car was produced by Lionel). The specialized well cars had no floors in the center section. The outside frame of the car provided the support needed to allow the load to ride only a few inches above the rails, **20**. This allowed A-C engineers to design machinery at the maximum size possible. Allis-Chalmers also operated a 12-axle depressed center flatcar for transporting extra-large electrical transformers and nuclear reactor parts, **5**.

The massive Allis-Chalmers loads were bolted to the decks of the depressed-center flatcars. Wooden timbers were wedged between the load and the end stops. Steel rods with shock absorbers braced the load to the tie-down brackets on the deck of

16 In the 1850s the Erie Railroad was built with a 6-foot track gauge. By 1880 the railroad had finished converting to standard gauge, which resulted in unusually high and wide clearances along its original right of way. This gave Erie a competitive advantage for attracting the movement of oversize loads. This ad from the October 1956 *Trains* magazine features a six-axle depressed-center flatcar loaded with an 18-foot-tall, 110-ton Westinghouse transformer. *Kalmbach Media*

17

Segments of a solid-propellant rocket motor ride on cushion-underframe 60-foot Santa Fe flatcars. Wood blocking and heavy threaded steel rods anchor the wide load to the flatcar deck. The car includes "Excess Width" and "Do Not Hump" placards. *Aerojet-General Corp.*

A Chicago & North Western engine picks up two open flatcar loads of solid rocket booster casing segments from Ladish Drop Forge in Cudahy, Wis., in December 1990. Ladish produced these specialty forgings for NASA's Space Shuttle program. *Greg Mross*

The Allis-Chalmers plant switcher, SW1 no. 8, is ready to pull a flatcar from the transformer shop at West Allis, Wis., in November 1985. Large pieces of hardwood blocking and threaded steel rods secure the load. Radiators are loaded on a second flatcar on the right, while workers prepare wiring for the next transformer.
Ed Wilkommen collection; Lake States Railway Historical Association

the car. Steel bracing was also used to secure the loads. Some of these eye-catching oversized loads included the manufacturer's name and logo with the slogan, "Allis-Chalmers Machinery for Good Living," as well as "Do Not Hump" signs, **21**.

Allis-Chalmers manufactured rotary cement kilns, which could be up to 500 feet in length. A typical kiln shipment was divided into five sections that averaged 100 feet each and measured 15'-6" wide. About once a year the Milwaukee Road handled a special train from West Allis to the Northwestern Cement Company at Mason City, Iowa. Due to concerns about clearances, the 10-car train only moved during daylight hours and at a maximum speed of 25 mph. The movement was carefully coordinated to safely move the kiln during the five-day journey.

Not all electrical equipment needed to be loaded on a depressed center flatcar. Circuit breakers, **22**, smaller transformers, **23**, and other electrical switching gear were loaded on conventional flatcars when possible.

I wanted to model a variety of loads for these depressed-center flatcars, but I wanted the loads to be removable. This was accomplished by placing a sheet of .015" styrene under each load. All securements, dunnage, and the piece of machinery were attached to this sheet. The base was wedged between the end stops on the lower deck of the car to keep it in place. This allowed for an easy exchange or removal. I found that loads requiring several steel rod supports reaching onto the upper decks were too delicate and needed to be permanently affixed to the car. Special equipment such as depressed center flatcars are kept in good condition, so they have minimal weathering, **24**. The decks are a lightly rusted color with scars showing the locations of previous welds. These marks are represented on the models with thick rust-colored paint applied with .015" wire.

When planning and creating model loads, I stay away from extremely wide or high dimensional loads because these cars create problems when operating on modular or club layouts. Just like the prototype, each model railroad has its limitations for clearance—use your judgment.

Allis-Chalmers well car ACMX 400 arrives in Mason City, Iowa with a new cement kiln tire for the Northwestern States Portland Cement Company in May 1965. The well car allows tall loads to ride as little as 2.5" above the railhead. When loaded, these cars were often restricted to 25 mph. *Clark Probst collection*

20

21

A rotary kiln segment manufactured by Allis-Chalmers passes through Burnham Yard in Milwaukee in October 1970. This high and wide load is reinforced and anchored to a six-axle, two-truck Chicago & Eastern Illinois depressed-center flatcar by wooden wedges and steel rods. Two bearings were added to the left side of the car to balance the weight of the load laterally. *Keith Kohlmann collection*

22

An Allis-Chalmers BZO-HV oil circuit breaker is bolted to the deck of a Pennsylvania class F30 flatcar at Joliet, Ill., in 1958. The electrical cabinet is braced with 2x4 blocking underneath. The glass electrical insulators are wrapped with heavy paper and tape. Radiators are wrapped, taped, blocked, and banded to the deck. *Bruce K. Meyer*

Wind turbine loads

Giant windmills—wind turbine generators—began appearing in great numbers in the U.S. in the 1990s. Most of the wind turbines installed in North America have been built from components manufactured in Europe, but increasingly the blades and towers are being manufactured domestically to save on shipping. Depending on the location of the wind generation project, the parts will be moved by rail. European parts are trans-loaded from ships to rail or trucks at coastal and Great Lakes ports.

Each component of a windmill is handled differently. Transformers are shipped on heavy-duty depressed center flatcars, **25**. Tower sections and rotors are carried in fixtures on dedicated flatcars, **26**. The nacelle contains the generator and other mechanical components, making it quite heavy. One nacelle is loaded into a fixture mounted on each bulkhead flatcar. Blades can be up to 180 feet long. They are a single piece, lightweight, and quite delicate. Protective racks support the blades. These stay with the blades when they are unloaded from the ship onto the flatcar. Blades loaded on flatcars

23

This transformer is held in place on Soo Line no. 5150 with wooden cleats on the deck and chains with links and turnbuckles locked into the side sill channels. The load includes radiators, cooling oil in barrels, and other equipment protected by wooden blocking nailed and strapped to the deck. It's in Minneapolis in July 1980. *Jim Podlich*

This N scale Micro-Trains model has been lowered and lightly weathered to represent a Pennsylvania F35 125-ton depressed-center flatcar built in 1940. The boiler section load was made from an oil tank and a part from the scrap box. Basswood bracing was cut to fit the round shape. Styrene represents the steel bracing. *Keith Kohlmann*

25

Several Elin 250-ton transformers have been transferred from a ship to heavy-duty depressed center flatcars at the Port of Milwaukee on April 16, 2005. The transformers were imported from Europe as part of a large wind-energy installation in Iowa. *Keith Kohlmann*

Wind turbine rotor hubs rest on steel support fixtures welded to the deck of QTTX 132025 at Duplainville, Wis., in April 2011. Plastic wrappings protect the mating surfaces where the blades will connect to the hubs. Chains with tensioners secure the load. *Keith Schmidt*

Wind turbine blades require unique mounting fixtures that allow them to pivot on curves. Each blade occupies two flatcars. Special unit trains move the blades over long distances to staging areas where the blades are transferred to trucks. These are on the Union Pacific at Pueblo, Colo., in 2013. *Frank Orona*

and accompanying idler cars travel from ports to the unloading sites in dedicated trains, **27**. The fixtures are usually made from unpainted steel, while the aluminum, fiberglass, and composite windmill parts have a matte appearance.

Several model manufacturers have produced windmill parts, fixtures, and flatcars in several scales. There are also people making and selling the windmill parts they make on 3D printers (do an online search). These parts convert existing flatcar kits into windmill loads.

Airplane components

Airplane components are often built at factories some distance from their final assembly locations, and are often shipped by rail. The best-known and most visible of these operations began in 1966 when Boeing started building fuselages for its 737 aircraft at a plant in Wichita, Kan. The plant, acquired by Spirit AeroSystems in 2005, still ships the bodies via rail to Renton, Wash., for final assembly, **28**. These were initially shipped in sections aboard 50-foot flatcars, but the fuselages now travel assembled atop BNSF-owned 89-foot flatcars equipped with special cradles. The cars, with a trailing idler flat, have bulkheads to protect the ends of the fuselage from damage; some idler flats include built-on enclosures to carry additional components. In 2013, 35 fuselages a month were making the 1,800-mile journey.

Components such as wings and stabilizers also travel by rail. As high-value items, they are covered for shipment. Since the late 1960s, these are often handled in custom containers called Skyboxes, **29**, **30**. These containers have top hoods that can be lifted off, enabling easy loading and unloading of large components. The Skyboxes are high/wide loads and travel on specific, assigned routes. Through the 1980s, these were often painted with their manufacturer or subcontractor's paint schemes and lettering.

Industry modeling

A massive industrial plant could be a model railroad unto itself. An easier approach that saves space is to only model the interchange tracks and loading areas around the edges of the plant. The plant's huge shops and warehouses could be hidden from view, or modeled as flats or backdrops, with the open loads demonstrating the activity taking place beyond the edges of the layout. Another option is to build the shops double-sided, with switching locomotives passing through doorways picking up and delivering cars on both sides of the buildings. Large shop buildings can be used as view blocks that separate different areas around the factory complex. Use your imagination, and let your modeling interests direct how you model both the cars and industrial areas.

A Boeing 737 fuselage atop BNSF 800123 pauses at Balmer Yard in Seattle in November 2019 en route to Renton, Wash., for final assembly. The green aluminum fuselage was manufactured by Spirit AeroSystems in Wichita, Kan. Protective shields at both ends of the two-car set deflect obstructions. *Bob Bender*

Skyboxes were designed to carry aircraft wings and stabilizers. A new Southern Pacific car is at San Diego in 1965 (above). At right, a crane sets the Skybox cover in place on a Santa Fe car that's just been loaded with wing sections for a C-130 at Lockheed's Burbank, Calif., plant; it will soon be on its way to Lockair, Ga. The containers, atop 53-foot flatcars, stood 19'-6" above the rails.
Above: J. David Ingles; right: Santa Fe

CHAPTER FIVE

Buses, trucks, autos, and other vehicle loads

Three new Railway Express Agency step vans ride on Milwaukee Road 66240, a 53-foot flatcar, at DeKalb, Ill., in 1960. The wheels are secured with wood blocking nailed to the deck. Four strands of wire are looped between each wheel and a stake pocket, then twisted tight with a wooden stake. The stake can still be seen in the wires. The wires run under the axles in an "X" pattern. *F.R. Ritzman Collection, Lake States Railway Historical Association, Baraboo, Wisconsin*

We've looked at construction equipment, but many other types of vehicles are also shipped by rail, including trucks, buses, automobiles, trailers, wagons, and delivery vans, **1**. Small railroad locomotives and rolling stock, such as streetcars, industrial locomotives, and narrow-gauge and export locomotives, also often travel aboard flatcars.

Four flatcar loads of commercial horse-drawn moving vans are ready for shipment from the Racine-Sattley wagon company in Racine Junction, Wis., in 1905. The wheels are blocked on all sides by cribbing that also goes through the spokes to secure the wheel. Neither chain nor wire was used to secure the load. The shipment includes four 30-foot painted canvas signs advertising the company's products. *Racine Heritage Museum Archival Collection*

A pair of Fruehauf semi-trailers is en route from Detroit to Des Moines, Iowa on a Rutland flatcar around 1918. The wheels are blocked and the axles and ends are braced. The trailers rest on their noses rather than on their landing gear. All wheels are secured with cribbing and a wire looped through the spokes and stake pockets. Note the fancy pinstriping on the wheels and trailer sides. *Doug Harding*

New wagons and carts have been moving by rail for delivery to customers in distant cities and on the fringes of the rail network ever since railways started operating, and new trucks and highway trailers and bodies continue to do so today. Just as we see enclosed tri-level auto racks in freight trains today, open flatcars loaded with new wagons and carriages are the 19th century equivalent, **2**.

In the first two decades of the 20th century, automotive technology advanced quickly. Horses and steam power were rapidly replaced by internal-combustion engines in cars, trucks, and tractors. New automobiles were largely hidden from view, shipped

Workers stack the top layer of crated Nash automobiles on a Chicago & North Western wood-sided gondola at Kenosha, Wis., on Nov. 20, 1928. The wooden crates contain partially disassembled autos for export. The crates were covered with canvas banded around the top to keep the loads dry during overseas shipment. Identifying information was stenciled on all sides of each crate. *Archives of the Kenosha County Historical Society*

Six new right-hand-drive mail delivery trucks for the U.S. Post Office ride on Trailer Train flatcar ATTX 470893 in July 1965. The trucks are secured to the deck with chains. The 75-foot former piggyback car, built in the mid-1950s, was converted in the early 1960s to carry vehicles. *J. David Ingles collection*

Three Elgin White Wing sweepers are loaded on an Elgin, Joliet & Eastern flatcar at Council Bluffs, Iowa, in October 1974. The sweepers are secured using twisted wire and wheel blocks. *M.D. McCarter N12973*

inside double-door automobile boxcars equipped with interior loading racks. Trucks and larger vehicles were placed on open flatcars, **3**. Autos and tractors destined for export markets were shipped in kit form enclosed in protective wooden crates for ease of stacking and to conserve space inside the holds of ships, **4**. The wheels and tops were removed and packed inside a crate to make the boxes as compact as possible. Nash exports to Australia, for example, were the chassis only. The wooden and sheet metal bodies were fabricated locally. The export boxes of vehicles and machinery traveled from the factories to the ports inside gondolas.

Although loaded on a piggyback flatcar, these stainless tank trailers were not in revenue service. The brand-new trailers were on their way from the Fruehauf plant to their buyer in the early 1960s. The car is an 85-foot Trailer Train car with collapsible trailer hitches. By the early 1960s, railroads found that these hitches alone (which locked to the trailer kingpin) were sufficient to secure trailers without additional tie downs. *John Ingles; J. David Ingles collection*

From general-purpose flatcars to Trailer Train

Vehicles loaded onto flatcars must be firmly and properly secured to counteract the forces exerted upon them while in transit. The weight and speed of trains places a great deal of stress and strain on the loads. Slack action slams loads forward and back in a longitudinal direction as trains brake and accelerate; lateral rocking forces push loads outward on uneven track and on curves. Vertical forces on uneven track can bounce loads and cause great damage. All of these forces are compounded by rough track and harmonics. As mentioned throughout this book, the American Association of Railroads' loading rules were created through intense testing and are proven to work.

For most of the 20th century, AAR loading diagrams for solid and rubber-tired vehicles required wooden blocks around the wheels. The blocks were nailed to the wooden deck of the flatcar. Four strands of annealed steel wire were looped around or through the wheels and tied through the stake pockets. The wires were twisted until they held the load tightly, **1**.

The AAR bracing techniques allow for differences among various types of vehicles, but all wheeled vehicles were blocked and braced in essentially similar ways. All used chocks of one pattern or another to keep the vehicles from moving. All used wire or cable, in varying combinations, to help vehicle

A new N scale Texaco fuel tank trailer is posed for a photograph outside The Heil Co. factory in Milwaukee, Wis. The flatcar is a modified Red Caboose model loaded with a Trainworx tank trailer. The wheels were blocked with basswood. Twisted EZ Line was used to tie the load to the stake pockets, and "Do Not Hump" signs were added to the deck. This scene was inspired by a clip from an Association of American Railroads promotional film from the 1940s. *Keith Kohlmann*

bodies resist longitudinal, transverse, and vertical forces. Wooden blocks nailed at the front and back of wheels kept vehicles from moving lengthwise on the flatcar. Cleats or boards nailed along the inside or outside of wheels prevented centrifugal force from shifting or flinging vehicles off the car on curves. Wire tightened between wheels and stake pockets reduced bouncing.

In the 1960s a new method for securing vehicles was offered by Trailer Train (which had provided piggyback flatcars since 1956). The new flatcars were longer and provided increased loading capacity. Chains that were part of the equipment assigned to each car secured the vehicles (see photo in "Tie-down chains" in Chapter 2, page 36). In addition to offering general service flatcars, Trailer Train had flatcars geared to carrying equipment for specific loads. Tie-down chains, machinery fixtures, supports, and auto racks were assigned to flatcars ranging from 60 to 89 feet in length. Wooden blocking and twisted wire were no longer required. However, strapping and wire rope continued in use as secondary tie-down material, **5**.

General-service flatcars owned by individual railroads continued using wooden blocking and twisted wire through the 1990s. This method became less common as TTX pool

Four new HO scale International semi tractors (from Walthers) travel on an 86-foot Athearn flatcar. This well-detailed load, modeled by Dave Sima, is secured to the car with wire looped over the axles and through the deck of the car, which gives the appearance of the chains used by the prototype. No weathering was used on the trucks, making them appear factory-new. *Keith Kohlmann*

10

Freight motor M16 of The Milwaukee Electric Railway & Light Co. eases a Milwaukee Road flatcar up to the 20th Street team track in Milwaukee in November 1938. The flatcar carries a new Yellow Coach electric bus, no. 139. The wheels are chocked with wooden blocking. *Keith Kohlmann collection*

11

Edmonton Transit Service no. 174 is a Brown Boveri electric bus that has returned to Edmonton after being on loan to the Toronto Transit Commission. It's riding on an OTTX flatcar and spotted at the team track ramp in Strathcona Yard at South Edmonton, Alberta, in December 1993. The bus is riding low because its air suspension has been drained for the cross-Canada journey. The wheels are blocked and the bus is chained down. *Keith Kohlmann*

12

Fifteen new 1964 Ford Mustangs leave Detroit on RTTX 910546, an 89-foot tri-level open autorack. The rack is secured to the Trailer Train flatcar. Racks were owned by the railroads participating in pools of cars (in this case, Detroit, Toledo & Ironton). The automobiles are secured to the rack with chains built into the decks. *J. David Ingles collection*

Bi-level auto racks carry taller vehicles that require additional clearance, such as these GMC vans on the Milwaukee Road in March 1973. The Penn Central rack is mounted atop a Trailer Train flatcar. *Keith Kohlmann collection*

13

14

Mini-vans assembled in Ontario ride aboard CN 710100, a Canadian National 89-foot bi-level auto rack, in June 1999. The vans are partially protected from rocks by side screens. *Keith Kohlmann collection*

15

Santa Fe no. 176709 is a class GA-61 gondola specially equipped to haul auto frames. The end frame bracket supports two rows of leaning frames. An adjustable frame clamps down on the far end of the frames to secure them; it's connected to the side braces. The frames fit into rows of wooden slats on the floor. It's at San Bernadino, Calif., in 1958.
K.B. King, Jr.; Lloyd Keyser collection

Truck frames roll on the Norfolk Southern through Danville, Ky., on Aug. 19, 2018. These flatcars are assigned to frame service, and have special racks that move with the car. There is no waste dunnage. When the car is empty, the tie-down equipment is stored in bins at the end of the car. *Bob Bender*

equipment increased in number and variety, but many loads were still secured using the wire-down technique, **6**. Purpose-built flatcars for piggyback (trailer-on-flatcar) service began appearing in the mid-1950s, with trailer hitches on the platforms locking the trailers in place. Although that service is beyond the scope of this book, piggyback flatcars were also used to deliver new trailers to customers, **7**.

Whatever the flatcar type, the type of vehicle(s) riding on it is particularly helpful in defining the era and location of the modeled scene. Vehicles reflect changes in technology and style in a way that can harmonize with the style and technology seen in surrounding structures and railroad equipment on a layout. Model manufacturers offer vehicles of all types and in all scales to match nearly any time or place, **8**, **9**. The type of vehicle load can be matched to the type of flatcar designed to carry it. Compare the 50-year difference in automotive styling shown in the images of electric buses from different eras in **10** and **11**. The railroad equipment and the styling of the vehicles both help define the two eras.

Trailer Train changed the way finished automobiles were shipped. Through the steam era, autos were hidden from sight, riding in double-door boxcars that, with interior loading racks, could each hold four automobiles. This method of loading and shipping were very labor-intensive and inefficient, and by the late 1950s the trucking industry could deliver cars to dealers faster and cheaper—trucks had captured more than 90 percent of this traffic by 1960.

The coming of tri-level auto racks on Trailer Train 89-foot flatcars—which could carry 15 autos—in 1960 brought the majority of this traffic back to railroads, **12**. Larger vehicles, like pickup trucks and vans, rode on bi-level racks, **13**. It was the start of a 30-year period where loads of colorful vehicles were common, and prominently displayed as they rode on their auto racks. Built-in tie-downs (chains with hooks on ratchets) secured the autos in place.

Although this new equipment was a success, the finished vehicles were exposed to bad weather, rock damage, theft, and vandalism—problems that grew worse by the 1970s. The railroads' initial solution was to add various types of side panels on their auto racks during the 1970s, **14**. Ultimately, the best solution was completely enclosed auto racks, which began arriving in great numbers by the 1980s. Colorful rows of new automobiles are no longer a part of the railroad scene.

Automobile and truck frames are often produced at locations distant from assembly plants. To increase efficiency in shipping them, railroads by the 1940s were equipping flatcars and gondolas with racks to ship the frames nesting and standing on end in two parallel rows, **15**. In the modern era, the frames are stacked flat on

17 **An open load of N scale frames is about to be spotted at a manufacturing plant. Pere Marquette no. 18692 is a modified Micro-Trains gondola with a 3D printed automobile frame load from Shapeways.** *Keith Kohlmann*

18 **Bethlehem Steel no. 5, a 50-ton diesel-electric industrial switcher built by Whitcomb (a division of Baldwin) passes through DeKalb, Ill., in 1946. The locomotive is secured with steel straps and wood blocking. The headlights and exhaust stack are covered with cardboard and tape.**
Ritzman Collection, Lake States Railway Historical Association

19 **This General Motors narrow-gauge export locomotive is completely wrapped in plastic sheeting in August 1986. Heavy hardwood cribbing under the bolsters supports the load. Threaded steel rods are anchored through the stake pockets to the locomotive. Chains secure the plastic covering. The trucks follow on the next flatcar.** *J.R. Quinn*

20 **An Indonesian Railways CM20EMP locomotive, built by General Electric, is one of several export locomotives traveling together through Conway, Pa., on May 26, 2013. Hardwood cribbing and chains secure the loads. The locomotives were shipped without trucks, which were manufactured in the Indonesian Railway's shops.** *Paul Wester*

custom-equipped TTX 89-foot flatcars. Specialized tie-down equipment stays with these cars, **16**. Until Nash began building unibody cars without frames in 1941, all U.S. automobiles were built on frames, and open loads of frames traveling to assembly plants across the nation were very common. Today the major brands build only unibody cars. Certain trucks are still built on frames, but auto frame flatcars have become rare. Several model companies offer kits for auto frames that can be used as loads on flatcars or gondolas, **17**.

Locomotives

Small industrial locomotives, export locomotives, narrow gauge (steam and

An EMD locomotive carbody rolls through Deval Junction at Des Plaines, Ill., in May 1989. It was built in London, Ontario, and is on its way to La Grange, Ill., for assembly. Temporary internal steel bracing and wood blocking keep the carbody straight. Polyester straps secure it to the OTTX flatcar. *Vince Kotnik*

diesel) locomotives, and electric transit cars cannot be shipped by rail on their own wheels. The gauges or couplers might not match, and rough handling might damage the equipment, **18**. Many locomotives are placed on flatcars for safe movement over long distances, with trucks removed and placed on the another car if the vehicle is too tall, **19**, **20**. Unfinished locomotive bodies are also shipped to final assembly plants by rail, **21**.

These are usually secured with blocks, steel rods, and cables in the same manner as heavy equipment. Passenger car bodies being shipped are often loaded aboard flatcars equipped with bolster adapters, **22**. These adapters can be moved on the flatcar deck to match the length of the carbody being carried. They lock to the car's bolsters, securely holding them while eliminating risk of damage to gear under the car floor.

Modeling these loads provides opportunities to showcase equipment that wouldn't normally fit into your usual model railroad operating scheme. An old streetcar might be passing through on its way to a museum, **23**, or new equipment for a distant railroad could pass through. Port facilities can see just about any kind of machinery or vehicle appear in open loads on the docks (both inbound and outbound).

This stainless-steel gallery car for Chicago's Metra commuter service was one of 150 manufactured in Japan by Nippon Sharyo, Ltd. and moved by ship to the Port of Savanna, Ga., in 2003. The JTTX flatcars are equipped with bolsters that lock the carbody in place for the trip to Super Steel in Milwaukee for final assembly. Each car was covered with a thick quilted blue cover (see the car in the background at right). *Dave Nelson*

Carmen from the Chicago & North Western adjust the steel rods securing North Shore coach 727 to a Milwaukee Road flatcar at North Chicago, Ill., in February 1964. Stub stakes, bracing around the trucks, and wedges under the wheels keep the car in place. The interurban car, built by Cincinnati Car in 1926, was in 1963 purchased by the Iowa Chapter of the National Railway Historical Society for excursion service on the Southern Iowa Railway.
Ed Wilcommen Collection, Lake States Railway Historical Association

CHAPTER SIX

Forest products and building materials

Center-beam flatcars were developed in the late 1960s and are now the most common way of carrying dimensional lumber and sheet goods. Ratchets are built into the side sills, with cables passing over the lumber and connecting to the center beam. This Burlington Northern car is loaded with 45 bundles of 12-foot-long 2x8 boards. The car is designed to handle five stacks of 12-foot bundles (or a combination of standard lengths) to fill its 60-foot inside length.
Jeff Wilson

Forest products shipped by rail in open cars fall into several groups: logs, finished lumber, **1**, plywood, treated poles, ties, pulpwood, wood chips, and stumps. Products vary in their sizes and requirements for safe handling, resulting in a wide variety in the size and type of the freight cars used to transport the loads.

This Milwaukee Road log flatcar carries 11 logs to a sawmill in 1978. This modern, 42-foot, welded all-steel car was built for this purpose. Heavy stakes support the logs, which rest on large steel bunks. This arrangement allows the car to be loaded and unloaded by a wheel loader equipped with forks and a grapple. Steel banding keeps the load from shifting. Paper tags help identify the load at the mill. *Keith Kohlmann collection*

This modern 100-ton capacity bulkhead flatcar carries a full load of hardwood logs at Sunbury, Pa., in May 2002. The car has permanent side stakes with five chains running across the top of the load. *Ruben S. Brouse*

Logs

Railroads provided an economical solution to the challenges of moving logs from forests to distant sawmills. Both private logging companies and common-carrier railroads built branch lines into forested areas to extract the logs. Logging railroads were built as both standard and narrow gauge lines in many areas of North America. The tracks were usually abandoned when the resources ran out.

Standard flatcars with side stakes and skeleton flatcars were the most common types of equipment used in the woods. Standard flatcars and gondolas could also be used. Logs on flatcars were secured with stakes and banding or chains. However, their wooden decks were quickly destroyed by the pounding of the logs, so steel skeleton log cars were preferred, **2**. As freight cars became larger, 60-foot bulkhead flatcars with permanent side stakes have become the norm. These cars can be easily loaded and unloaded with heavy equipment, **3**. Most log hauls were fairly short—often under

4

A Texas & New Orleans 52-foot drop-end gondola serves as a log car at Jasper, Texas in 1958. Steel stakes attached to the inside of the car, with chains across the top, contain two piles of 20-foot logs heading for the sawmill.
K.B. King; collection of Lloyd Keyser

5

A Chicago & North Western wood gondola is being unloaded on a siding in 1919. Four 2x6 posts nailed to the inside of the car support the stack of lumber on each side. The load shifted while in transit, and no spacers were needed between bundles of lumber because these loads were stacked by hand. *C&NW Historical Society Archives*

Workers are in the process of transloading lumber from a standard gauge Southern Pacific boxcar to a narrow gauge flatcar on the Nevada County Narrow Gauge at Colfax, Calif., in April 1939. Side stakes and twisted wire will be used to secure the load. *Bill Schaumburg collection*

100 miles from the logging area to a nearby mill.

Specialty logs (rare or highly desired wood) being shipped to distant mills or furniture factories were placed inside steel gondolas. If cars were loaded so that at least half of each log was below the top edge of the gondola, chains or banding were not needed. Side stakes were used where the load extended above the side of the gondola, **4**.

Christmas trees were shipped on flatcars and in gondolas. The trees were wrapped in burlap and tied with twine, then piled flat on the deck of the car. A wire was looped between opposite side stakes to hold down the load. The cars were unloaded at team tracks or house tracks near commercial districts. Some dealers sold the trees right off the car at the team track.

Lumber

Lumber is one of the most basic and versatile building materials. It has been shipped by rail since the 1840s. Early sawmills cut logs into thick planks that were shipped to lumberyards where they were re-sawn and planed into the dimensions needed to meet local demands. As transportation, communication, and milling equipment became more advanced, lumber was cut to standard dimensional sizes and dried at the mill before being shipped to lumberyards.

Lumber has been shipped in boxcars, gondolas, **5**, and flatcars. Through the steam and early diesel eras, boards were loaded by hand into the cars, **6**. Individual boards were tightly stacked on the floor of the car. At 2-foot intervals, strands of wire were wrapped around the boards to create a bundle. Separator sticks were

This view from October 1966 illustrates the way lumber was commonly loaded on flatcars through the 1960s. Boards were piled on spacers, then banded together. Side stakes were wired or banded, then framed with 2x4s. Note that the load is asymmetrical, and there are gaps within the load. These loads were prone to shifting while in transit. *Keith Kohlmann collection*

A Duluth, Winnipeg & Pacific bulkhead flatcar arrives at Butler, Wis., in April 1988 with a full load of 2x4s imported from Canada. The 2-foot-thick bundles are individually banded and separated with spacing boards. Different bundle lengths are staggered throughout the load. The car has no center beam, so the bundles are also tied to each other across the car for stability. *Vince Kotnik*

9

A lumber bundle has shifted badly on this 61-foot Southern bulkhead flatcar. Bulkheads prevent shifting longitudinally, but not laterally. Center-beam flatcars solved this problem. The car has been switched from its train; its load will be restacked and the car sent on its way. *Vince Kotnik*

placed on top of the bundle, and another bundle of boards was built on top of the first bundle. Each bundle was wired or banded to the one above it. Three or four wooden 4x4 side stakes braced each stack of bundles. At the top of the stack of bundles, the side stakes were supported laterally and longitudinally by 1x4s nailed to the stakes. This framing secured the load. Flatcars usually held two or three stacks of bundles, with each stack independently secured to the car. Lumber could also be stacked this way in wood-side gondolas that had stake pockets. This was a very labor-intensive method of loading lumber. Slack action often shifted boards toward the ends of the flatcar during shipment; vibration and slack action created a ragged-looking pile after a long journey, **7**.

By the mid-1960s loading of lumber was mechanized. Lumber was strapped together into bundles with high-tension banding that could be handled by a forklift. This allowed for larger loads and tighter packing. The bundles were placed on 2x4 spacers along the deck of the flatcar. Straps

10

A Clark C55s 11,000-pound dual-drive LPG-powered forklift removes a bundle of eighty 14-foot 2x10s from a center-beam car at the Kuiken Brothers Company in Succasunna, N.J., on Jan. 15, 2020. The spacers have milled channels to accommodate the polyester straps, which maintain the bundle and spacers as a single unit. *Bill Schaumburg*

11

A Soo Line center-beam car passes through Railside, Alberta in July 2015, with a load of lumber wrapped in polyethylene plastic. The cables on this car wrap from the side sill to the center beam and secure the load tightly. The protective plastic wrappers are rolling billboards for the lumber mills. *Keith Kohlmann*

Bundles of wet veneer are en route to a plywood manufacturing facility in 1972. The bundles are strapped together and braced inside the car. Long side stakes pass through the roof to keep the load inside the car. The old Milwaukee Road welded rib-side car had its double doors removed and side stake pockets added. Door openings at least 10 feet wide were needed for loading the veneer. *TRAINS magazine collection*

An open load of 25-foot poles rides in a Pennsylvania 46-foot drop-end gondola near Chicago in 1944. The poles are arranged with the tips overlapping at the center of the car to help keep the load level. Unpeeled saplings are supported by twisted strands of wire to keep the poles from shifting. *C&NW Historical Society Archives*

An N scale load of treated poles rides in Denver & Rio Grande Western no. 72268, a Trainworx GS gondola model. The poles are dowels that were tapered by sanding, then stained by wiping them down with Minwax wood finish penetrating stain. They were glued into a solid block, with styrene stakes and banding glued directly to the load to make it durable and removable. *Keith Kohlmann*

secured the bundles to one another and the stake pockets. This was called a "floating load" and did not need wooden side stakes for support. The ends and sides of the stacked bundles were braced by 2x4s nailed into the wooden deck of the flatcar. Bulkhead flatcars became popular to better stabilize lumber loads, **8**.

Even with improved banding methods, the impact forces of slack action and rocking could shift the load and loosen the tie-downs, causing boards to stick out beyond the ends of the car. This creates a hazardous condition. Open lumber cars are occasionally set out en route to have a shifted load adjusted and re-secured by the car department, **9**.

To combat issues with shifting loads (and to carry larger loads allowed by increasing weight limits in the 1960s), the center-beam car emerged, **1**. Center-beam cars are specialty flatcars designed to carry bundles of dimensional lumber, sheet goods, and building materials. They began to appear on North American railroads in the late 1960s and by the late 1980s became the dominant method to ship lumber. The cars have 60- or 73-foot interior lengths between their bulkhead ends, with a center beam, or wall, running down the center of the car between bulkheads. This beam is a structural support for the car and also provides support for the bundled loads. The cars are equipped with cable tie-down ratchets built into the side sills. The cables wrap around the bundles, and the ends are secured to slots in the center beam. After the car is emptied, the cables are re-secured diagonally to the center beam. Permanent spacers along the floor allow the tines of a forklift truck to reach under the bundles. A center-beam flatcar must be loaded and unloaded symmetrically to keep it from becoming unbalanced and tipping over. A consignee must have a level surface where the car can be unloaded from both sides, **10**.

Plastic-wrapped packaged lumber became common in the 1960s. Today most finished lumber rides in wrapped or partially wrapped bundles on bulkhead flatcars or center beam flatcars, **11**. Rough-cut and treated lumber can be left partially exposed to the elements, but high-value finished lumber is still shipped in boxcars to protect it from moisture.

Lumber operations

Lumber loads are shipped directly to a lumberyard, wholesaler, or end user (such as a furniture factory), and loads can travel long distances (often cross country). Through the 1960s, mills commonly shipped carloads of dimensional lumber before the load had a buyer. The consignee was a lumber broker who searched for a buyer while the car was in transit. Slow, circuitous routes were often chosen for these shipments until a buyer was found; the railroads essentially became a warehouse on wheels for the brokers. This method of shipment included many interchanges between railroads at remote junctions across the

15

This 42-foot Frisco flatcar carries treated poles from the American Creosote Works of Pensacola, Fla., in 1959. Steel bands wrap the load of 25-foot poles. But the unpeeled saplings in the stake pockets (note where they've been trimmed to fit) were unable to prevent the load from shifting significantly—it started off centered on the car. *J. David Ingles collection*

country. Short lines and freight-hauling interurban railroads gained significant revenue handling this lumber between interchanges. Many large railroads maintained designated sidings in yards at certain points along the route for the unsold lumber. The railroads provided this service through a separate tariff, which included extra switching and car use. The broker had 14 days to sell the load while in transit. These carloads were called "roller lumber." As soon as the load was sold, the car was re-directed for delivery to the buyer through regular freight service. Some modelers replicate this pattern of car movement in their operations.

This method of shipping was eventually outlawed, and by the 1980s, regional reload centers appeared. A reload center is little more than a large paved area for unloading, storing, and reloading bundles of lumber to be shipped out by rail or truck (many reload centers handle a variety of other products and materials as well). A buyer can order a custom variety of

A multiple-car shipment of 91-foot pressure-treated (creosoted) utility poles is at Phoenix, Ariz., in February 1988. Idler flatcars are placed at both ends of the 65-foot drop-end mill gondolas to protect the overhanging poles. Side stakes made from branches and peeled logs are reinforced by steel banding running across the tops. More banding ties the creosoted poles together at several points. The mill gondola at right has permanent steel side stakes. *Dave Nelson*

16

This bulkhead flat with log bunks is leased by Redwood Rail LLC. The load of creosote-treated poles, secured with polyester straps, is passing through Lake Bluff, Ill., in May 2018. *Keith Kohlmann*

grades and dimensions of lumber and have the mixed bundles placed in a single shipment. These reloads can be recognized by a mix of bundle logos from several mills seen on a single car. Loads direct from the mill have only one logo on the bundles.

Wet veneer

Stacks of large sheets of peeled veneer were banded together and shipped in open boxcars to plywood factories in the Pacific Northwest. Rows of three bundles about 36" high each were stacked inside the boxcars, which had their doors and tracks removed, **12**. The lower track was replaced with three or four stake pockets. Side stakes ran from the pockets up through holes cut into the car roofs. These were older double-door cars with side openings that were 10 feet wide or wider. Only wet veneer was handled in open boxcars—finished veneers were shipped inside insulated boxcars to protect the load from moisture and temperature changes.

Plywood and sheet goods

Plywood is the best-known type of sheet good (building materials sold in sheet form). Sheet goods are a type of engineered wood that includes MDF (medium-density fiberboard), OSB (oriented-strand board), and chipboard (particle board). They are generally manufactured in 4 x 8-foot sheets or panels.

Plywood became popular as a building material around World War II. Initially, it was shipped in double-door boxcars to protect it from the elements. With the introduction of plastic-wrapped package lumber in the 1960s, wrapped exterior-grade sheet goods could be loaded onto bulkhead flatcars (and later on center-beam cars). However, moisture and temperature-sensitive sheet goods are still shipped in enclosed double-door boxcars. The logos of the manufacturers appear on the outer wrapping of the bundles.

Poles

Pressure-treated utility poles and pilings are a common wood product shipped by rail. Treated-pole production is of particular interest to modelers of open loads because each step in the production of poles requires different rail and industrial facilities. Cedar poles are primarily produced in the Pacific Northwest and western Canada. The mid-south region of the U.S. produces more than half the nation's treated poles, and they are all Southern pine. Other than increased mechanization, the process hasn't changed much over the last century.

Transforming trees into utility poles begins with selecting the right trees from a parcel of mature forest. Pole logs are of a high value; to avoid the chance of damage from having other sawn trees fall on them, they are the first trees to be cut. Once selected and felled, the trees are cut to lengths in multiples of five feet, usually between 25-45 feet, with 35 feet the most common. Some poles are longer, from 55 to 75 feet.

The logs are stripped of branches and bark where they fall and are skidded out. A century ago, this was done by horse or a steam donkey engine, giving way to tractors by the early 1900s. The logs were shipped on trucks or floated in booms to a landing site with a rail spur. At the landing, logs were loaded onto 40- and 50-foot flatcars or gondolas with a crane. Large wooden stakes lined the side pockets of the flatcars, and the stakes were wired together across the load, **13**.

In the modern era, 60- to 85-foot bulkhead flatcars and skeleton flatcars with permanent side stakes are used to move the poles. Poles are thinner at the top than the base, so to achieve a full and balanced load, poles shorter than the length of the flatcar are loaded with the thick ends placed at both ends of the car with the tips overlapping in the middle. Longer poles (40-50 feet) alternate directions on the flatcar for a level load. The longest poles (55-70 feet) are placed on top of shorter logs if they overhang the end of a car. An idler flatcar is placed next to the loaded car, but the pole does not rest on it. Long poles fit comfortably in modern bulkhead log cars, and an idler car is only needed with the longest poles.

The load is secured with stakes and steel wire or polyester straps. Side stakes are made from green saplings or 4x4 posts which are driven securely into the stake pockets, usually 4 or 6 per side. Strands of steel wire are run around the pole load at several levels in the pile to secure groups of poles together. Four strands of wire are looped around the tops of opposite side stakes. The wire is twisted tight to support the stakes. Cars are loaded up to the maximum weight capacity for the trip to the treatment plant, making the pile about 10 feet high.

Poles can be modeled from tapered dowels. Place a length of dowel in a power drill and run it against a sheet of 100 grit sandpaper to taper the end. I stain model poles with a mix of two parts boxcar red, one part roof brown, and four parts thinner; you can also use an appropriate color of stain from the hardware store, **14**.

At the treatment plant, logs are shaped to uniform dimensions. Some receive a thick coat of shiny black creosote on the bottom 4 feet of the pole, with a thinner treatment up to the top of the pole. Other poles are fully treated to the top for use as piles in bridge, building, and dock construction, **15**. Chemically treated poles come out with a green tint and no creosote.

To re-create the appearance of freshly creosoted poles, stain sanded dowels with thin washes of oily black or brown pant. Utility poles are usually lighter in color at the top, gradually getting darker to fully blackened at the base. Paint bridge pilings oily black. Drybrush the ends with clear gloss.

Finished poles are shipped in gondolas or flatcars to customers all over the country. Today the poles are mostly shipped in bulkhead flatcars equipped with permanent side stakes.

This Elgin, Joliet & Eastern gondola shows the method of using sapling stakes and wire mesh to secure a load of pulpwood on the Escanaba & Lake Superior in 1974. *Robert Ferge; Keith Kohlmann collection*

Milwaukee Road gondolas 4 and 80179 were in pulpwood service in northern Wisconsin in July 1972. These home-built cars were originally converted to haul steel pipe in 1958. The wooden sides were removed and the floor was replaced with open slats 2.5" apart. They served their final years in pulpwood service. Note how logs are placed vertically at the ends to serve as bulkheads and increase the capacity of the cars. *Keith Kohlmann collection*

20

In 1952 the Southern Railway operated 701 pulpwood rack cars in the 114000-114999 series. The cars were modified from obsolete truss-rod 36-foot boxcars, had a 40-ton capacity, and represented 75 percent of Southern's pulpwood fleet in the early 1950s. A J.I. Case Model LAI is shown loading these cars in North Carolina. The tractor was modified with a Harrison loader, pulpwood handling frame, and slings. *Racine Heritage Museum Archival Collection*

This Canadian Pacific bulkhead flatcar has been converted to a log car. Twelve permanent heavy steel stakes were welded to the side sills. This alternate-direction loading pattern helps stabilize the load. It's at Hayward Junction, Wis., in April 1996. *Bob Gallegos*

Polyester straps secure the load. Treated poles leaving the plant are not piled as high on the cars as the cedar logs were when coming in because they are heavier. A typical outbound flatcar or gondola load is seven to 10 poles high. Modern bulkhead flatcars can be filled to the top because they have a higher load limit. Several layers of banding tie the layers of poles to the stake pockets of flatcars and the tall untreated wooden stakes along the sides. Very long poles were often shipped in mill gondolas or on top of a load of shorter poles, overhanging an empty idler flat or another car loaded with poles consigned to the same location, **16**.

Banding on models can be simulated with monofilament thread or E-Z Line. Glue the separate poles together into a solid block with the banding running through the layers of poles, then glue the ends of the banding to the stake pockets on the car. To create removable loads, glue the banding to the bottom of the lowest pole and temporarily secure the completed load in place on the car with Elmer's or LePage's poster tacking material.

This Chicago & North Western boxcar is a former Rock Island waffle-side car in wood chip service at Waseca, Minn., in September 1996. Doors made of heavy paper and 2x6 boards hold the load in. The paper is cut to spill out the load at the mill. *Tom Ferrell*

Treated poles and pilings are shipped to signal departments and the bridges and buildings departments of railroads, construction companies, county and state highway departments, and telephone, telegraph, and electric utilities for installation along their service lines. These companies often have a material yard with a rail spur for receiving and storing material. Outlying local team tracks are also commonly used by utilities and contractors for unloading poles closer to the installation sites. Empty flats and gondolas weren't usually assigned to carrying poles exclusively, so the car could be loaded with some other commodity before being returned to its home road. Modern bulkhead flatcars with permanent side stakes usually operate in dedicated service and are returned empty to the shipper for another load, **17**.

Railroad ties

The wood for railroad ties is cut in the East, South, Midwest, and Northwest. In the past raw ties were shipped to and from the treatment plant in gondolas, but today they travel in center beam cars. Since the ties are solid wood, a center beam flat can only be loaded to a little over half full with railroad ties. Both treated and untreated ties are loaded level with the

Northern Pacific no. 119998 is a purpose-built wood chip car at Omak, Wash., in August 2005. The top-hinged door on the "A" end of the car for dumping the load is visible at left. Plastic netting covers the load to keep it from blowing out at speed. *Olev Taremae*

top of the gondola sides (see page 106 in Chapter 8).

Worn-out ties are loaded into gondolas or re-purposed steel rotary-dump coal cars. The ties are sold to a scrap materials dealer and are eventually either shipped to home improvement centers for use in landscaping projects or ground up and used as fuel. In the 1980s the CNW and other capital-starved railroads re-used ties taken from abandonment projects. The usable ties were simply flipped over and re-installed at other locations.

Used railroad tie loads can be modeled by roughing up wood or plastic ties with 50-grit sandpaper. Cut split ends into a few of the ties with a hobby knife. Use matte medium to glue the ties to the top of a filler block that brings the top layer of the load right up to the top edge of the gondola. Paint the load with railroad tie brown paint, followed by rust and dust. Tie-plate scars and spike holes can be drawn onto the ties with paint markers to add additional detail to the load. A gondola load of new ties can be modeled in the same manner, but use a black wood

Southern no. 289076 is an all-steel 50-ton general service (GS) gondola loaded with stump wood on its way to a turpentine still in Dallas in 1956. A load of stumps can be modeled with broken roots and shredded twigs. *Al Chione*

25

A Santa Fe 53-foot bulkhead flatcar is loaded with wrapped bundles of wallboard (plasterboard) in July 1964. The car is outfitted with a skeleton rack specifically designed to secure the wallboard; it was built by Brandon Equipment in conjunction with U.S. Gypsum and Santa Fe. *Santa Fe*

stain to color the ties. To replicate the look of fresh creosote, drybrush Testor's Oil and Grease to the tops and ends of the ties.

Pulpwood

Pulpwood is timber too small or not high-enough quality to be used as dimensional lumber. It's shipped by rail from load-out sidings in forest areas to paper mills. Generally speaking, gondolas are used in the Northeast, Midwest, and Canada for pulpwood service. Bulkhead flatcars are used in the Southeast.

When loading gondolas, the logs are cut and stacked to fit across the width of the car. If the gondola is not equipped with bulkheads, then a row of vertical logs is placed across the ends of the car to create a wall that supports the load on each end, **18**. Many railroads welded permanent bulkheads and side supports into 40-foot gondolas for pulpwood service. This was a common modification that sped loading and increased the capacity of older, otherwise-obsolete equipment. Some shippers wrapped the sides of their pulpwood loads with wire mesh to prevent logs from falling out of the cars, **19**.

Pulpwood branch lines in the upper Midwest were notorious for rough track and falling logs. Crews had to stay alert for logs protruding from passing trains. Once a year the Chicago & North Western, for example, operated a work extra along these branch lines. The train was equipped with a hydraulic grapple mounted on a gondola, and several gondolas were filled with recovered pulpwood logs.

Bulkhead flatcars used by railroads in the Southeast often transport shortwood—logs 6 feet long and under. They are stacked in double rows on the V-shaped deck of the flatcar. Gravity helps keep the logs in place. These cars are designed specifically for hauling short pulpwood.

Wallboard today often rides on center-beam cars. This 73-foot GAEX car carrying wallboard from LaFarge is equipped with wide straps instead of the steel cables usually found on these cars. The straps are less likely to damage the wallboard. It's at Rochelle, Ill., in 2007. *Jeff Wilson*

This former Ashley, Drew & Northern bulkhead flatcar is loaded with fiber cement board at San Pedro, Calif. The wrapped sheets are banded to pallets, and the rows of stacked pallets are banded to the stake pockets. This heavy material filled the car to its weight capacity with only three layers of bundles. An airbag was inserted between the pallets to press the load tight against the bulkheads. *Bob Gallegos*

In the 1940s the Southern Railway, Illinois Central, Louisville & Nashville, and others converted obsolete truss-rod box cars for pulpwood service by removing the roof, sides, and the upper half of both ends. The remaining ends became bulkheads, **20**.

Modern bulkhead log cars are modifications of older bulkhead flats. The wooden decks are removed and tall, permanent side stakes are welded to the cars. Logs can be piled longitudinally, laterally, or an alternating pattern of both, **21**.

Pulpwood loads can be modeled by cutting twigs of an appropriate diameter to length, then gluing and stacking them in the car. To make a load removable, first line the car with a plastic bag before gluing the sticks together with matte medium. After the glue dries, peel away the plastic bag to reveal a load that will fit perfectly in the car.

Wood chip cars

Through the steam era, wood chips were hauled in a variety of open hoppers and gondolas as well as boxcars. Much railroad traffic is

Missouri Pacific no. 8553 is a modified 48'-6" flatcar in palletized brick service. The MP equipped these flatcars with bulkheads and removable side panels. Brick is heavy; a full load isn't very tall. The car awaits unloading at the J.H. Haumersen & Sons brickyard spur in Racine, Wis., on Aug. 27, 1965. *Clem Devine*

seasonal, so any equipment that was not in demand was used to haul wood chips. Temporary wooden doors (grain doors) covered the lower three-quarters of boxcar door openings. Wood chips were blown in through the upper opening above the grain door. Beginning in the 1950s, temporary doors made from heavy kraft paper reinforced with steel banding replaced the wooden grain doors.

Some railroads re-purposed older composite-side boxcars for wood chip service by removing the doors and cutting an opening in the roof for loading. Many older steel boxcars spent their last years in wood chip service from the 1970s through the 1990s, **22**. Some paper mills operated private fleets of wood chip boxcars.

Loaded wood chips were visible through the opening above the door. This can be modeled by first removing the sliding doors. Cut a block of foam that fills about three-quarters of the car. Glue fine sawdust to the top of the block with matte medium. Install pre-printed grain doors from Jaeger Products or make your own generic doors from brown kraft tape. Glue strips of basswood across the door opening or draw horizontal lines across the doors with a fine-tip marker to replicate the wood or steel reinforcement found on some paper doors. Glue the paper doors to the sides of the block to cover the door opening. Insert the block snugly into the boxcar body. Some wood chip boxcars had an open door on only one side. Others had openings cut into the roof for loading. A good article on the subject was "Modeling Paper Grain Doors," in *N Scale Railroading*, in November-December 2009.

As the demand for wood chips increased in the 1960s, older three-bay open-top hopper cars and gondolas that were no longer needed in coal service were equipped with side extensions to increase the capacity of the cars. Wood chips are not as dense as coal or stone, so side extensions allowed carrying a larger load.

Modern wood chip cars are 65-foot or longer bathtub gondola or hopper cars built specifically for hauling chips, **23**. These have tall sides and can have either smooth sides or exterior posts and bracing. The cars can be equipped with either rapid discharge bottom dump doors or a hinged end door. With these, the car is raised on a special car dumper at the mill to pour the chips out through the open end door. Wood chip hoppers in mainline service are covered with a fine mesh net which keeps the chips from blowing out while allowing moisture to escape from the load. These loads can be replicated with a foam block, matte medium, and fine sawdust. Cover the load with white extra fine tulle netting.

Wood chip gondolas are also used to ship cottonseed from Texas to large cattle feeding operations in the Midwest.

Stumps

In the southeast U.S., shredded pine stumps, roots, and slash are collected

A finished fabricated home is secured to a Rock Island flatcar in June 1964. Its wheels are blocked and the frame is chained to the stake pockets. Wooden props support the hitch end of the frame. Notice how the load has the same height and width profile as the adjacent freight cars. *J. David Ingles*

after a pine forest is logged. The collected wood is stacked in gondolas and shipped to turpentine stills to produce raw gum turpentine, gum rosin, and pine tar for the wood chemicals industry.

Stump cars were gondolas heaped with a mud-covered riot of shredded stumps and roots, **24**. As unruly as these loads may have appeared, there were rules for loading them. Half of each stump should be loaded below the top edge of the gondola, with the large end down along the outside rows. Stumps in the center row could not stick up more than half their length above the outside row. No material could overhang the sides and ends of the car.

Several southern railroads operated dedicated gondolas in this service. Seaboard Air Line used special 41-foot steel gondolas that had 6" slots cut through each side panel at the floor line. This was done to help facilitate cleaning bark and dirt out of the car after it was unloaded.

A stump load could be modeled with small broken sticks taken from bushes or fine roots. The more fibrous and shredded the branches, the more realistic the load will look. These stumps were very gnarled and twisted, which makes this type of open load so compelling. The load should be weathered with mud-colored paint. The sides of the gondolas could also be covered in mud and rust.

Construction materials

Flatcars were used (and sometimes modified) to handle the specific needs of different types of non-wood building materials. Gypsum wallboard (plasterboard) became a popular interior building material in the 1950s. Railroads used bulkhead flatcars to handle pallets of wallboard, which were stacked in bundles. Heavy plastic tarps were wrapped around the loads to keep them dry; some cars had specialized racks to keep them secure, **25**. By the 1970s, wallboard was often carried on center-beam cars, again with bundles wrapped tightly to keep out moisture, **26**; the material often rides in boxcars as well.

Bulkhead flats also carry other building materials, including cement siding, **27**, shingles (and other sheet roofing material), rigid insulation, and shipments of palletized bricks, **28**.

In the 1960s complete manufactured homes were sometimes shipped long distances on open flatcars. Wausau Homes, Marshfield Homes, and Rollohomes were manufacturers who used railroads to deliver their products. These homes were designed to fit within standard railroad clearances. Oversized homes were shipped in subassemblies and were handled as wide loads. The open sides of the homes were covered with plastic sheeting to keep out the rain. Mobile homes required wooden bracing under the frames, blocking around the wheels, and four tie-down chains, **29**. Homes could be secured to TOFC flatcars by locking them to the trailer hitch and blocking the wheels.

CHAPTER SEVEN

Military equipment

An 89-foot Grand Trunk Western flatcar carries two HEMTTs (Heavy Expanded Mobility Tactical Trucks) at Milwaukee in June 1988. The trucks are on their way from the factory in Oshkosh, Wis., to a U.S. Army base for delivery. Chains in two lengthwise channels on the deck secure the vehicles. *Vince Kotnik*

Since the advent of railroad transportation, military units have taken advantage of the speed and relative ease of moving men and materiel by rail overland to ports, bases, and battles. The United States Army Transportation Corps was formed in 1942 and is the second-largest branch of the Army. The Corps is headquartered at Fort Lee, Va., with railway training for reserve soldiers and Army civilian employees at Fort Eustis, Va. The motto of the Corps is "Spearhead of Logistics."

Military equipment is constantly moving by rail, **1**. These loads are leaving for maneuvers, going overseas, traveling to new posts and depots, **2**, or to maintenance facilities. Section 6 of the AAR manual, "Rules Governing the Loading of Department of Defense Materiel On Open Top Cars" from 1960 outlines the procedures for securing open loads for the military. To give you an idea of the scope and tremendous variety of these loads, Section 6 is 110 pages long and illustrates how the most common items are loaded on standard wood-deck flatcars and gondolas. Among other things, the manual shows how to load howitzers, anti-aircraft guns, cannons of all sizes, rocket launchers, barges, trailers, boats, landing craft, pontoons, buildings (Quonset components), marine buoys, jet and rotary engines, aircraft components, landing mats, paving equipment, Jeeps, tractors, armored cars, semi-trailers, motorcycles, amphibious landing vehicles, tanks, half-tracks, and 16-inch gun barrels. This information was for use by railroads, manufacturers, those

2

Representatives of the Massey-Harris Tank Division pose with M10A1 tank destroyers that have just arrived at the Racine Junction, Wis., plant. From June to December 1944, M-H rebuilt 500 M10A1s into M36 tank destroyers by upgrading the 75mm gun turret with a 90mm gun and cast-steel turret. The tanks were attached to the flatcars with four steel tie rods secured between the lift lugs and steel plates placed under the deck, 4x6 stub stakes with 2x4 blocking beside the tracks, and heavy 4x12 bracing at the end of each track. The gun was in an elevated position for the photo; normally the barrel would be lowered into the travel lock, similar to the other tank destroyers in the photo. *Massey-Harris*

An M577 CPC (Command Post Carrier) is chained to a TTX flatcar in the foreground. Two six-axle DODX flatcars carry four M270 MLRS (Multiple Launch Rocket Systems). The heavy-duty flatcars feature adjustable tie-down chains embedded in the deck to secure many types of equipment, and they do not require wooden blocking. It's at Galesburg, Ill., in June 2002. *Dave Nelson*

This USAX 54-foot, 100-ton heavy-duty six-axle flatcar was assigned to the Transportation Corps around 1960. Steel rods anchor the M48 tank to the stake pockets. Wooden blocking at the ends of the tracks and around the road wheels keep the tank from rolling. The turret is reversed, the barrel is in the travel lock, and it is tied with a cable to keep it from moving. The gun mantelet is wrapped with canvas. On Equipment Material (OEM) boxes contain tools, gunsights, and periscopes. The box is covered with a tarp and sealed with three steel bands. Three more steel straps and wooden 2x4s secure the box to the deck. *J. David Ingles*

who purchased army surplus material, and all branches of the military, **3**. These rules by and large follow the same basic principles as other heavy equipment, but the specialized nature of military equipment creates many variations.

Rail transport is essential especially for shipping oversize and overweight military equipment, and deployment of any equipment transported farther than 400 miles. Rail transport of tactical vehicles reduces the time the vehicles must operate during deployment, reduces wear and tear, minimizes en-route support, and reduces maintenance. Oversize and overweight military equipment is commonly transported by rail along

Chicago & North Western SD40-2 no. 6842 leads a westbound military extra up the center express track at Elmhurst, Ill., on Dec. 15, 1989, just one month before the counter-assault of coalition forces in Kuwait and Iraq. *Bob Baker*

established routes that have the proper clearances. Not all highways and bridges can accommodate these loads, and long convoys via highways require a lot of personnel to operate, are disruptive to other traffic, and require support along the way. Military rail shipments are often done as dedicated trains, operated as extra movements.

Not all shipments of cargo covered by these rules were for the military. In the decade after the end of World War II, many tracked and wheeled vehicles were sold to manufacturers who converted the equipment into civilian construction and logging machinery. Much of this heavy Army surplus was shipped by rail.

By 1953 the Transportation Corps operated a vast fleet of standard flatcars. In addition, it operated 780 heavy-duty 100-ton capacity flatcars. These cars had six axles and could move tanks and other heavy equipment over lightweight rail and bridges, **4**. A variety of Corps- and railroad-owned flatcars could be seen in trains moving equipment to ports for overseas deployments, to and from bases for National Guard training, and routine maintenance movements.

As Trailer Train equipment became more prevalent in the 1960s and '70s, it was used to transport military loads.

In this military movement at Galesburg, Ill., in 2003, the first two loads consist of (nearest to farthest) M109A6 Paladin 155mm Self-Propelled Howitzers and FAASVs (Field Artillery Ammunition Support Vehicles). The third and fourth flatcars carry a HEMTT (Heavy Expanded Mobility Tactical Truck) and an M113A3 armored personnel carrier (or similar), followed by a pair of M3 Bradley IFVs (Infantry Fighting Vehicles). Heavy chains secure the vehicles to the channels in the decks of the cars. *Dave Nelson*

7

Newly manufactured Joint Light Tactical Vehicles (JLTVs) pass through Pewaukee, Wis., on Dec. 26, 2020. The trucks are manufactured at Oshkosh, Wis. The trucks are secured on TPDX 190616 by four heavy chains locked into channels in the steel deck of the car. *Keith Schmidt*

8

Northern Pacific flatcar no. 6575 is returning an Oshkosh runway snow plow truck to the U.S. Air Force at the Delaware & Hudson Pine Street Yard in Schenectady, N.Y., on Feb. 28, 1971. This plow had just been remanufactured by the builder. Wooden blocking nailed to the deck and steel wire tied through the wheels and stake pockets hold the truck in place. Note the front plow rotation of 90 degrees to keep the truck from becoming a wide load. *Keith Kohlmann collection*

This New York Central flatcar carries ST-2145, a 45-foot steel-hulled small harbor tug built for the U.S. Army Transportation Corps in 1953. It was later transferred to the U.S. Army Corps of Engineers and re-named *Shelter Bay*. Heavy wooden cribbing and ¾" steel rods anchor the boat to the car in 1960. The propeller is blocked with 2x4s. *J. David Ingles*

Overseas logistics began to re-focus on containerized intermodal shipments, but large military vehicles are still moved by rail on a mix of cars owned by the U.S. Army, TTX, and individual railroads, **5**.

Armored personnel carriers are shipped on a variety of commercial chain-equipped cars. However, the M2/M3 Bradley can be easily shipped only on HTTX cars and Department of Defense (DODX) 41000-series and similar cars. These cars are equipped with channels for locking down heavier ½" chains. They don't have raised grab irons that would be crushed by the tracks during circus-style loading. The DODX 41000-series flatcars are 100-ton cars and can carry just one M1 tank. The DODX 40000-series 140-ton heavy-duty flatcar can transport two M1 tanks.

Modeling military open loads creates the opportunity to replicate specific equipment from a particular era. The loads could be new vehicles leaving the factory, a shipment arriving at a port, army surplus equipment, scrap loads, or a complete train of National Guard equipment headed to training or deployment, **6**.

There is a wide selection of military models available in all scales that can be loaded onto a variety of flatcars to match the desired era. Remember that paint, insignia, and camouflage patterns define the era modeled. New equipment being delivered generally doesn't show prominent insignia. Before 1975, most U.S. military vehicles were delivered in a single shade of olive drab, with camouflage and insignia added after delivery or deployment.

In August 1975, standard camouflage patterns with a regional color variety were adopted. Plans can be found in the manual TC 5-200 *Camouflage Pattern Painting*. NATO camouflage standards were adopted by all NATO countries in 1985. Tanks and vehicles with a standard sand-colored base coat have been prominent on military trains during the last three decades of war in the Middle East, **7**. (Many publications and online sources can provide specific details for determining proper paint jobs by era and type of equipment.)

Military tanks and armored vehicles are not shipped with machine guns mounted, **8**. This would expose the armaments to the elements and cause damage, and the guns would also be subject to theft and misuse. Likewise, missiles and rockets are not loaded into launchers for shipment.

Military vehicles are generally shipped in good or new condition, **9**. They might be a bit dusty, but not muddy, weathered, or damaged. Almost any type of vehicle can be shipped by rail for re-deployment or maintenance, **10**. Vehicles returning from overseas deployment must have all the soil washed off before returning to the U.S. to comply with Department of Agriculture regulations.

There are many reliable historical books and magazines available to answer specific questions about individual loads. The internet and railroad photo sellers can also provide useful information. Prototype photos are a great source of modeling ideas.

CHAPTER EIGHT

Maintenance-of-way and railroad service

This 41-foot gondola is known as a Stork Car. It's a dedicated car that carries the "Jimbo" materials handler, shown here peddling ties along the Chicago & North Western right of way at Belgium, Wis., in June 1997. Obsolete gondolas and flatcars were often converted to haul MofW equipment. *James H. Yanke*

Railroad cars in maintenance-of-way (MofW) service have been part of railroading since the first rails were laid 175 years ago. Once the first tracks were put down, flatcars and gondolas carried rails, ties, and other track material to extend the line. Railroads began reserving cars for MofW forces, who not only repaired track to keep it in operating condition, but also engaged in the constant process of upgrading the track structure as technological advances brought increasingly heavier trains.

A Milwaukee Road flatcar carries an Alco all-welded replacement steam locomotive boiler. It's on display for the public to inspect in January 1948. It will be installed on a class S-2 4-8-4 Northern at the railroad's Milwaukee shops. Wood blocking supports the firebox and cradles the boiler; steel rods wrap around the boiler from stake pockets on each side. *C.P. "Chappie" Fox*

As railroads expanded, new investments were made in communication and signaling equipment, stations, heavier bridges, yards, engine servicing facilities, new rolling stock and locomotives, interlocking plants, heavier rail, and ballast. Most of the materials for these projects were moved by rail as open loads to construction sites or shops.

The railcars used for this were once commonly old or obsolete freight cars rebuilt for the service, but since the 1970s it's become more common for cars to be built specifically for MofW service. Railroads use their own cars for on-line moves of this material; they're often painted and lettered specifically for MofW service (numbers will have an X or MW prefix or suffix), or wear special paint (Union Pacific MofW cars, for example, are green). However, cars making deliveries of materials (ties, rails, wheelsets) across other railroads will be standard revenue cars—albeit often specially equipped for the service.

Through the steam era, heavy

Cinders from steam locomotives and stationary boilers were a common gondola load through and even after the steam era. Here a company-service Chicago & North Western Hart Convertible gondola carries cinders in Madison, Wis., in 1964. Cinders were used as fill, roadbed, and ballast in yards and industrial tracks into the 1960s; they were also used for running tracks and other purposes. The sides on this gondola hinge outward, allowing easy dumping of loads. *Lloyd Keyser*

Workers dump limestone ballast along the Simmons Spur at Sheridan Road in Kenosha, Wis., in 1939. Chicago & North Western no. 96295 is a Rodger-Hart Selective ballast hopper, with bottom gates allowing dumping to either side or between the rails. These cars could also be used in revenue service hauling sugar beets or coal. The horizontal line on the center of the car says, "Load limit for crushed rock, sand or gravel" indicating the maximum height of the load for those commodities. *C&NW Historical Society Archives*

steam-powered cranes were used to construct track, bridges, and buildings. They were also used to repair cars and clear wrecks. Damaged equipment was placed on flatcars and shipped at a slow speed in "hospital trains" back to shops for repair. Wooden cars were often reduced to splinters in a wreck, but steel cars could be salvaged and repaired. Open and covered hopper cars needed to be protected when shipped without their trucks, so railroads developed adjustable bolster cars to safely carry wreck-damaged cars on open flatcars without having to rest the cars on their bottom bay doors.

Most railroads no longer use their own heavy cranes. Wreck recovery and cleanup is handled by contractors who serve multiple railroads. Rail grinding, undercutting, spreading ballast, laying fiber optic lines, brush clearing, and rail defect detection are now done largely by nationwide contractors.

Railroads are in a constant battle against elements, damage, and time. Floods, snowstorms, rock slides, erosion, hurricanes, and wildfires threaten to close lines; extreme cold

Cumberland Mine no. 1, an EMD SD38-2, picks up a loaded ballast car near Spraggs, Pa., in 1990. The simple but efficient loading ramp is used by a wheel loader to load the cars. United States Steel operated this isolated railroad between a coal mine and a dock on the Monongahela River. *Bob Gallegos*

A Chicago & North Western (ex-Rock Island) ballast car is being loaded with C&NW's signature "pink lady" quartzite ballast at Rock Springs, Wis., in August 1983. Each type of local ballast has its own distinct coloration, which can be represented in model form to make unique loads. *C&NW Historical Society Archives*

Side-dump gondolas have been in use since the early 1900s. They are commonly used in maintenance-of-way service, carrying fill, rip-rap, crushed rock, sand, and ballast. Large pneumatic cylinders raise the bed, while the side door drops to dump the load of rocks and clay clear of the track. *James H. Yanke*

Replacement rails are being unloaded from a Milwaukee Road composite-side GS gondola in front of the depot at Wauwatosa, Wis., in 1938. The steam-powered American cranes ride on permanent rails installed on the deck of the flatcars in work train service. The cranes are anchored to the ends of the flatcars with threaded steel rods when traveling long distances. *C.P. "Chappie" Fox*

A Chicago & North Western American locomotive crane pulls a G31 gondola in MofW service past the South Milwaukee, Wis., depot in July 1990. These cars were used to carry scrap rail and ties and thus did not need a floor. They were not used in interchange service. The car was fourth-hand to the CNW by way of Conrail, Penn Central, and the Pennsylvania Railroad. *Keith Kohlmann*

This Chicago & North Western (ex-Rock Island) gondola carries old railroad ties. New ties will be stacked evenly and neatly; old ties are often piled haphazardly, but below the top of the sides. They will sometimes be banded together. *Trains magazine collection*

This Union Pacific flatcar is equipped to carry concrete ties. Spacers separate the layers of ties; steel-frame bulkheads at each end help secure the load. The UP paints its MofW equipment green. It's on UP's main line in Nebraska in October 2003. *Jeff Wilson*

A Chicago Great Western flatcar has just arrived at Manitowoc, Wis., with three new Jackson Utility Tampers consigned to the Soo Line in 1966. The equipment is secured with blocking and twisted wire. The car rode the C&O carferry across Lake Michigan from Ludington, Mich., where the Jackson factory was located. *J. David Ingles*

A BNSF flatcar carries a two-layer load of wheelsets in 2016. The car has built-in cradles for each bottom-level wheelset, which are carried in staggered fashion. Lettering specifies "Two-tier loading, freight car wheels only." The "R-age" lettering indicates the car is in restricted service, online only, because of its age. *Jeff Wilson*

can snap rails; ballast and roadbed settle with operation, rain, and seasonal frost heaves; accidents damage pole lines, signals, and bridges; diamond crossings and switch frogs wear out with operation and need repair and replacement.

Into the 1950s, large gangs of maintenance-of-way employees kept the trains running. Local crews were based every few miles along main lines, each responsible for maintaining their section of track. This work was largely done with hand tools, and remained relatively unchanged through the end of the steam era. In order to lower operating costs, larger railroads were often the first to adopt mechanized maintenance-of-way machines. By the 1950s, diesel-powered hydraulic machinery replaced steam-powered cranes and hand labor. In the 1970s hi-rail trucks replaced speeders and local section gangs. Today's maintenance gangs work with highly specialized machinery year-round across dozens of states.

Looking back at the photos of crews building the Union Pacific main line for the first transcontinental railroad 150 years ago, it is amazing to think that each rail and tie was carried and laid in place by hand. Today the Union Pacific operates completely mechanized maintenance-of-way equipment. The newest tie pickup trains operate with incredible speed and are unmatched for their efficiency (see page 110). The four trains currently in operation are an essential part of Union Pacific's effort to replace

This flatcar was converted by the Chicago & North Western to transport wreck-damaged and bad-order cars back to the shop for repair. It has raised bolsters adjustable to a variety of truck spacings, allowing cars to be shipped without damaging brake gear and other underbody equipment. The damaged cars are secured with adjustable chains, eliminating the need for wooden blocking. It's at St. Paul, Minn., in June 1990. *John Luckfield*

An old 8,000-gallon, 40-ton class ARA II tank car heads for scrapping in a Pennsylvania gondola in August 1963. No effort was needed to protect brake gear and other under-frame components; the tank car body was simply placed in the gon, with the trucks at the far end. It was owned by R.J. Roesling and Co. *John Ingles; J. David Ingles collection*

between 3 million and 5 million ties annually. These interesting trains integrate all the engineering advances learned from more than a century of shipping open loads by rail. The trains have self-loading capability, built-in tie down equipment, a self-unloading off-track vehicle, LED lighting, GPS, PTC (Positive Train Control), and the ability to operate under any conditions in any part of the country, year round. A closer look at the Relco Tie Pickup train is an exciting look at the future, and a fitting way to end our examination of open load technology and how to model it.

The remaining photos throughout this chapter show MofW and materials cars with a variety of loads, from specialized equipment to ballast to wrecked cars to ties. They're just a small sample of the many potential modeling projects that exist for railroad service loads.

Crews watch as a pair of Canadian National cranes hoist the remains of a cylindrical covered hopper into a mill gondola at Oliver, Alberta on Nov. 13, 1990. Crawler loaders had punched holes in the side of the car to unload its fertilizer load before the car was lifted into the gondola. Some wrecked cars are cut up on the spot, while others are shipped back to railroad shops for repair or scrapping. *Keith Kohlmann*

Illinois Central Gulf flatcars carry damaged Wisconsin Electric Thrall steel coal gondolas to shops for heavy repairs after a wreck in on the ICG in March 1980. Note the missing rotary coupler and torch-cut side of the upside-down car, which is secured with heavy steel banding. *Keith Kohlmann*

This N scale wreck load was made by taking an older Roundhouse (now Athearn) Thrall gondola and warming it slowly under a heat lamp to reproduce the look of a bent freight car. Underframe details and a dummy rotary coupler were added. The wreck-damaged side panel was cut out and weathered with rust-colored paint. The car was glued to an Atlas flatcar, with heavy E-Z Line representing the steel banding. *Keith Kohlmann*

The last car of this Union Pacific tie gang MofW train carries a ramp. When the train is in position, the ramp is lowered by the Pettibone Speedswing, allowing it and all the other wheeled vehicles on the train to unload circus-style at a grade crossing. The ramp, the Speedswing, and all other vehicles on the train are secured to stake pockets or floor channels with chains. It's at Racine, Wis., on May 27, 2020. *Keith Kohlmann*

A 1960s-era 53-foot GSC cast-steel flatcar now in MofW service carries a Union Pacific tie-gang boom truck. It's chained to stake pockets fore, mid, and aft, and its wheels don't require chocks or blocks. Piggyback-style ramps at the ends of each flatcar allow equipment to self load and unload from the back of the train. *Keith Kohlmann*

Union Pacific no. 958500 MW is an EMD SD40-2 locomotive remanufactured by Relco of Albia, Iowa into a PU3200A-6. It powers a maintenance-of-way tie pickup work train at Racine, Wis., on Aug. 9, 2020. It was placed in service in May of that year. *Keith Kohlmann*

The UP tie pickup train uses two Caterpillar 325F L compact radius excavators to load used ties and debris into open cars. The patented Relco bogie system allows it to travel on integrated rails along the tops of the MofW cars. Bridge rails are placed between cars to provide a continuous track for the tie handling cranes. The crew can fill about 10 cars per day (around 5,000 ties). The sides of the cars are equipped with LED lighting for night operation. *Keith Kohlmann*

Union Pacific no. 958501MW has an operator's control cab, crew quarters, generator set, and a turntable with ramp for a crew-cab pickup truck. The ramp can be turned and lowered at a grade crossing or access road to load and unload the truck. *Keith Kohlmann*

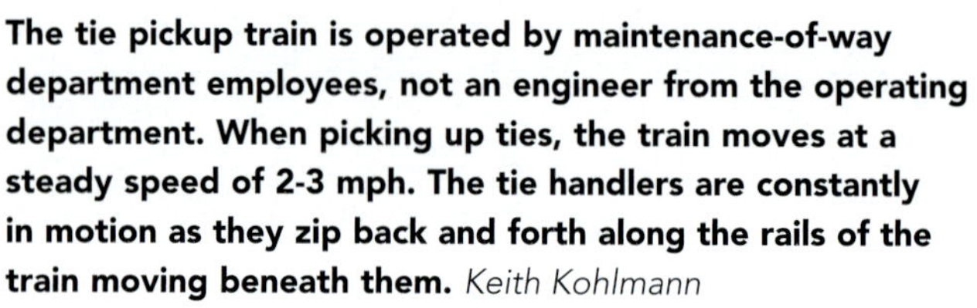

The tie pickup train is operated by maintenance-of-way department employees, not an engineer from the operating department. When picking up ties, the train moves at a steady speed of 2-3 mph. The tie handlers are constantly in motion as they zip back and forth along the rails of the train moving beneath them. *Keith Kohlmann*

Bibliography

Books

25 Freight Car Projects, Edited by Randy Rehberg. Kalmbach Publishing Co., 2016

America's Driving Force—Modeling Railroads and the Automotive Industry, edited by Laura Sebastian-Coleman. Wm. K. Walthers, Inc., 1998

Freight Cars of the '40s and '50s, by Jeff Wilson. Kalmbach Publishing Co., 2015

General Rules Governing the Loading of Commodities on Open Top Cars, by Operations and Maintenance Department—Mechanical Division, Association of American Railroads, 1963

Industries Along the Tracks, by Jeff Wilson. Kalmbach Publishing Co., 2004

Industries Along the Tracks 2, by Jeff Wilson. Kalmbach Publishing Co., 2006

Industries Along the Tracks 3, by Jeff Wilson. Kalmbach Publishing Co., 2008

Industries Along the Tracks 4, by Jeff Wilson. Kalmbach Publishing Co., 2010

Model Railroader's Guide to Freight Cars, by Jeff Wilson. Kalmbach Publishing Co., 2005

Modeling Open Loads, by A.C. Kalmbach Memorial Library. National Model Railroad Association, Inc., 2004

Modern Freight Cars, by Jeff Wilson. Kalmbach Media, 2019

Open Top Loads Flat Car and Gondola Color Portfolio, Vols. 1-4, by Robert J. Yanosey. Morning Sun Books, Inc., 2018

Postwar Freight Car Fleet, by Larry Klein and Ted Culotta. National Model Railroad Association, Inc., 2006

Trains, Tracks & Tall Timber—The History, Making and Modeling of Lumber and Paper, by Matt Coleman. Wm. K. Walthers, Inc., 1996

Periodicals

"Authentic Loads Enhance Operations," by Mont Switzer. *Model Railroader,* July 2010, p. 42-44

"Bucyrus: One Piece at a Time," by Keith Kohlmann, *Railroad Model Craftsman,* April 2006, p. 74-83

"Build a Realistic Flatcar Load," by Matt Snell. *Model Railroader,* December 2011, p. 48-51

"C&NW Burro Crane in N Scale," by Keith Kohlmann. *Model Railroader,* October 1999, p. 102-103

"Case History of Alvin Bowman," *Case Factory Eagle,* August 1949, p. 5-6

"Chains, Chocks, and Shackles," by Jim Hediger. *Model Railroader,* June 2005, p. 80-83

"Chicago Great Western 50-ton Flatcar with Bantam Trench Hoe Load," by Keith Kohlmann. *RailModel Journal,* January 2002, p. 62-64

"Crushed Automobile Loads for Dimi-Trains N Scale Gondolas," by Keith Kohlmann. *RailModel Journal,* June 2000, p. 53-54

"Detail and Add a Load to a Centerbeam Flatcar," by Pelle K. Soeborg. *Model Railroader,* October 2011, p. 47-49

"Easy N Scale Pole Loads," by Keith Kohlmann. *Model Railroader,* April 2004, p. 86-87

"False Floors Make Load Swapping Easy," by Jim Hediger. *Model Railroader,* June 2012, p. 22-23

"Flatcar Loading Practices—AAR Rules, Various Commodities, and Loaded Cars," by Patrick C. Wider. *Railway Prototype Cyclopedia,* Vol. 20, p. 1-85

"Freight Loads for Gondolas," by Ted Culotta. *Railroad Model Craftsman,* December 2005, p. 100-107

"HO Container Gondolas," by Jim Hediger. *Model Railroader,* March 2003, p. 47

"How to Model a Flatcar Full of Tractors," by Mont Switzer. *Model Railroader,* February 2016, p. 38-42

"How to Model Super-Size Loads," by Jim Hediger. *Model Railroader,* July 2008, p. 38-43

"ICG 50-foot Flats with Wrecked Thrall Gondola Loads," by Keith Kohlmann. *RailModel Journal,* October 2002, p. 8-10

"Loading of Materials," *Train Shed Cyclopedia,* Vol. 36, p. 1112-1113

"Lumber Loads from the 1940s and '50s," by Noel T. Holley. *Model Railroader,* June 1992, p. 79-81.

"Machinery Loads for Gons," by Clark Probst. *Railroad Model Craftsman,* March 2011, p. 48-49

"Model Realistic Stacked Steel Plates," by M.R. Snell. *Model Railroader,* March 2016, p. 58-61

"Modeling Flatcar Loads of the Bucyrus-Erie Plant," by Keith Kohlmann. *Railroad Model Craftsman,* May 2006, p. 74-77

"Modeling Paper Grain Doors," by Keith Kohlmann. *N Scale Railroading,* November-December 2009, p. 42-43

"Moving Monster Loads is a Railroad Specialty," by Jim Hediger. *Model Railroader,* March 2011, p. 22

"Mr. Hough's Loaders," by George Barrett. *Equipment Echoes,* Spring 1998, p. 23-28

"Never Just Scraping By… The Story of Caterpillar Scrapers Part I- The 1940's," by Roger Amato. *Equipment Echoes,* Spring 1998, p. 13-16

"Northwest Shovel Flatcar Load," by Keith Kohlmann. *N Scale Railroading,* May-June 2005 p. 44-45

"An N Scale Depressed Center Flatcar," by Keith Kohlmann. *Model Railroader,* August 2001, p. 76-78

"N Scale Flatcar Loads- Caterpillar's D8 bulldozer & No. 80 Pull Scraper," by Keith Kohlmann. *Railroad Model Craftsman,* December 2004, p. 72-76

"Pennsylvania Railroad F30A Class Flatcars," by Richard Hendrickson. *RailModel Journal,* April 1999, p. 26-28

"Pennsylvania RR F30E Flatcar," by Chuck Yungkurth. *Model Railroader,* November 1986, p. 106-107

"Simple Tarp-covered Loads," by Bruce Petty. *Model Railroader,* July 2008, p. 47

"Steel Loads," by Todd Sullivan. *Railroad Model Craftsman,* July 1982, p. 70-71

"Super-Size Loads," by Jim Hediger. *Model Railroader,* July 2008, p. 38-43

"Thirty-five Years of Trailer-Train- Pt. I," by Jim Panza. *Railroad Model Craftsman,* July 1990, p. 72-79

"Thirty-five Years of Trailer-Train- Pt. II," by Jim Panza. *Railroad Model Craftsman,* August 1990, p. 74-84

"Three Loads for Open-top Cars," by Cody Grivno. *Model Railroader,* October 2018, p. 26-29

"Trains and Tractors: The J.I. Case Plant in Racine, Wisconsin," by Keith Kohlmann. *Railroad Model Craftsman,* February 2012, p. 72-79

"TTX's 60-foot Flatcars," by Jim Panza. *Railroad Model Craftsman,* September 1997, p. 59-67

"USRA-Design 42-Foot Flatcars," by Richard Hendrickson. *RailModel Journal,* January 1997, p. 53-59

"Wabash 50-foot Gondola with Baled Scrap Load," by Keith Kohlmann. *N Scale Railroading,* p. 48-49

Miscellaneous

Highlights: Allis-Chalmers West Allis Works, 1955

Scrap is Fighting Metal, Institute of Scrap Iron & Steel, 1943

Tiedown Instructions for Rail Movements, SDDCTEA MI-19, Seventh Edition, Military Surface Deployment and Distribution Command, Transportation Engineering Agency. Scott AFB, Illinois, April 2015